THE COVID-19 SUPPLY CHAIN

Fact not Fiction

Hedley Rees

CONTENTS

PREFACE

This book is a sequel to a previous book titled *Taming the Big Pharma Monster by Speaking Truth to Power.* It was published on 28th May 2019. I wrote it as a companion book to a conference my company, PharmaFlow, hosted 8th May 2019, at Techniquest, Cardiff Bay, in South Wales.

The conference was titled *Medicines for the 21st Century: Safe, Better, Cheaper.* It came to life in the context of a rapidly increasing volume and intensity of calls for major reform of companies developing and supplying medicines into healthcare systems (pharmaceutical companies). The modus operandi of those companies appeared to be working against the best interests of those using their products – patients and healthcare professionals.

Accordingly, on May 8th, 2019, a group of clinicians, patients, representatives of relevant charities, experts in product development, legal, regulatory and supply chain specialists gathered together in Wales, with the aim of examining that claim, based on facts and evidence.

The day was organised in conference format. It involved in-depth dialogue and transfer of knowledge, over three panel sessions, between invited attendees and panel members, considering issues and opportunities in relation to safe medicines, better medicines, and cheaper medicines.

Emcee for the day was broadcaster Clare Forestier. The inauguration speech was given by former First Minister of Wales, Carwyn Jones, at the kind invitation of conference attendee Professor Keshav Singhal, CBE, a consultant orthopaedic surgeon with Cwm Taf Morgannwg Health Board and Chair of the British Association of Physicians of Indian Origin (BAPIO Wales).

The Keynote Address (pre-recorded) was given by Janet Woodcock, MD, then Director, Center for Drug Evaluation and Research (CDER), FDA.

Proceedings were recorded on video, and live polling was used to collect inputs from those in attendance.

Following the conference, I took all the contributions and wrote them up in a white paper. The paper went to the House of Commons Health and Social Care Committee (HSCCOM), Chaired by Jeremy Hunt MP at the time. Receipt has been acknowledged both by the Chair and the Committee Secretariat. Unsurprisingly, I've heard nothing since, as the world was about to change forever.

COVID-19 was poised to strike, and the intervening years have taken a punishing toll on society. A new breed of individual, identifying as a critical thinker, or medical freedom fighter, emerged from the fall-out. These individuals have been the spur for me to publish the book you are about to read.

My objective is to set the record straight when it comes to the true story on the development, manufacture, and distribution of medicinal products, with special reference to the SARS-CoV-2 injections. You may be relieved to know that what is to come is founded on solid facts and evidence. You may wish to challenge other versions of 'the truth' based on what you read here.

Hedley Rees, August 2023.

CHAPTER 1 ABOUT THIS BOOK

T his book is for the enlightenment of anyone wishing to learn more about pharmaceutical supply chains in general, and the COVID-19 supply chains in particular.

Prescription and over-the-counter drugs (drugs from here on) are the single biggest intervention in medical practice. The supply chains that produce them are the vehicle by which drugs get into your body. Once in, you cannot get them out.

The book aims to explain to you all the things you need to know about developing, producing, and distributing drugs in the supply chain—all written in an easy-to-understand fashion.

About You

You will be curious, someone who likes to ask questions and get answers based on facts and evidence. As well as being curious, you may well find the contents here useful in your chosen line of work or profession. That would include people working inside and outside the industry where a deeper knowledge of pharmaceutical supply chains will help them carry out their work more effectively.

Also, you may have been damaged in some way by pharmaceutical supply chains or wish to avoid being damaged in the future. There was a tragic event in 2007 where patients died and suffered serious adverse reactions, after a toxic material had been substituted for a genuine raw material in the supply chain for the blood thinner heparin. Readers can find this detailed in Chapter 7.

Despite intense activity between Governments, Regulatory Authorities and industry, there is nothing to prevent it happening again. That, and the issues of counterfeiting and diversion of cargo for illicit economic benefit, will be covered later.

Finally, you may want to get your questions on the COVID-19 response answered. Questions such as:

"Why did so many critical items go into short supply?"

"Why were over 90% of raw materials sourced from China?"

"What risk management plans were in place?"

Most tellingly "Who was in charge of it all?!"

What Should You Take Away From This Book?

What picture comes to mind when you think of pharmaceutical supply-chains?

* Not a single one?

* Lorries pulling up at the hospital unloading bay?

* Vans/trucks delivering into the pharmacy?

If those are mainly the pictures that come to mind, you should get a lot out of this book. There is much more to it than that.

That's only the tip of the iceberg. The journey through the various production stages, beginning with raw materials, sees drugs and their components travel tens, if not hundreds of thousands of miles. They go through multiple airports, seaports, countries, and continents. They are acted upon, handed over, acted upon again, handed over again…

…and so it goes.

The typical length, from beginning to receipt of the product in the pharmacy is 2 - 3 years. That is what is known as the cumulative lead-time. It means that the companies at the beginning (raw material producers) are producing materials for drugs that will be needed in 2 or 3 years' time.

The quantities they produce depend on projections, estimates, and forecasts. These are handed down from the companies along the chain. The company developing or selling the drugs at the top of the chain must start the ball rolling, based on sales expectations in their business plans.

When a seismic change in demand occurs, as with COVID-19, it is going to severely challenge the best of supply chains. When the supply chains have been neglected by their owners for decades, we get what we got; chaos and confusion.

This is an extract from a book I authored titled *Supply Chain Management in the Drug Industry, published by Wiley in 2011*:

Left unattended, supply chains lay around doing the human equivalent of lounging on the sofa, drinking pop (soda), eating sweets (candy), and watching TV. They behave like neglected children. No other sector seems to have neglected its (supply chain) children to the degree that pharmaceuticals have. The parents are now paying the price for all those years of neglect. The big question is: How do they get the children up off the sofa to start to become productive members of society?

In this book you are reading now, you will join me in getting under the skin of what has gone on in pharmaceutical supply chains. That will help you make informed decisions on the drugs you take, from a position of knowledge and understanding.

Why Listen To Me?

In Chapter 17 of the Wiley book, the final chapter, I made the following comment:

"In earlier chapters we expressed concern about the malaise that currently pervades pharmaceutical supply chains. The author [me] has a name for the condition. I have termed this serendipity induced chronic-disconnectedness, accompanied by change inertia (SICCI = sicky; please excuse the awful pun). The serious meaning behind this is that the frantic search to discover blockbuster drugs has resulted in a disconnected industry which in turn is disconnected from its supply chains. This, together with the continued belief that serendipity can form the basis of a sustainable business model, kills the will to change."

Although the book sold in 35+ countries, based on its content on professional management of the supply chain, the messages on the need for massive change for the better did not permeate to the right quarters—CEOs and investors in large pharmaceutical companies (Big Pharma).

Undeterred, I've continued to preach the important messages ever since, through publications, speaking at and co-chairing conferences, webinars, podcasts, and on LinkedIn (until I was ejected in August 2021).

In doing that, I seem to have acquired a dual identity in the industry. One is Hedley the consultant, working with companies who want the knowledge, understanding and strategy to help build their presence in the pharmaceutical supply chain. The other Hedley is attempting the impossible of taming the big pharma monster, by advocating and speaking on radical reform of the industry, for the benefit of all involved.

It is my strong belief that the more you, as a critical thinker, are informed on the workings of the machinery that will insert drugs into your body, the greater the chance of ending this nightmare. SARS-CoV-2 innoculations have been thrust upon the world with no consideration for the safety of those subjected to the medical procedure—it must be stopped, now.

Let's work on that together!

CHAPTER 2 INDUSTRY AND REGULATION

T here are two types of drugs produced in the industry:

- Small molecule - that means they are made using industrial chemistry. Aspirin is an example. The pharmaceutical industry was mainly founded on small molecule products.

- Biologics (large molecule) - biologics are essentially made from living things, such as animal and human cells. A monoclonal antibody is an example. There has been rapid growth of biologics in recent years.

There Are Two Main Business Models Involved:

- Innovators (originators) – these are companies that carry out the R&D and market small-molecule and/or biologic products.
- Generics/Biosimilars – these are companies that copy the original innovator products, either small molecule or biologic.

Regulatory Authorities

Drugs and their supply chains are regulated by a designated Competent Authority known as a Regulatory Authority.

- In the United States, the Regulatory Authority is the

> Food & Drug Administration (FDA).

- In Europe, the Regulatory Authority is the European Medicines Agency (EMA).

- In Japan, the Regulatory Authority is the Pharmaceuticals and Medical Devices Agency (PDMA).

Regulatory Authorities principally approve drugs for clinical trials and sale, inspect and license organisations and facilities for suitability to operate in the drug industry, and monitor the safety of medicines.

Regulations are laws, not nice to haves. Remediation of a breach is legally enforceable and may lead to prosecution. In the US it is the Federal Food, Drug, and Cosmetics Act, first passed in 1938. Similar legislation is in place in the EU under various EU Directives. The original directive title is shown below:

DIRECTIVE 2001/83/EC OF THE EUROPEAN PARLIAMENT AND OF THE COUNCIL.

There have been various amendments since to be found on the Eurpoean Medicines Agency (EMA) website.

UKs MHRA has to follow all EU Directives, even though it has left the EU, since this is required to allow UK-based pharmaceutical companies to sell into the EU.

Websites

In the main, Regulatory Authorities have comprehensive websites and should be your first source of reference for all matters regulatory.

If you are in a different region, an internet search engine should reveal the Regulatory Authority that applies to you.

International Council For Harmonisation Of Technical Requirements For Pharmaceuticals For Human Use

The International Council for Harmonisation of Technical Requirements for Pharmaceuticals for Human Use (ICH) has globally harmonized the drug evaluation and approval process, by introducing and agreeing a common template.

Licensing Drugs For Clinical Trials

An application to run clinical trials in humans is termed an Investigational New Drug (IND) application in the US.

For clinical trials in the EU and UK, it is termed a Clinical Trial Application (CTA).

The Clinical Trial Sponsor (CTS) is legally responsible for all the data and information submitted in an IND/CTA application. The detailed requirements for an IND can be found on the FDA or EMA websites.

The IND/CTA application must contain information in three broad areas:

- Animal Pharmacology and Toxicology Studies

- Clinical Protocols and Investigator Information

- Manufacturing Information [Supply Chain Information]. This is information pertaining to the composition, manufacturer, stability, and controls used for manufacturing the drug substance and the drug product. This information is assessed to ensure that the company can adequately produce and supply consistent batches of the drug.

Licensing Drugs For Sale

Applications to sell new drugs in the US are termed either a New Drug Application (NDA) for a small molecule drug, or a Biologics License Application (BLA) for a biologic product (SARS-CoV-2 inoculations are biologic products).

In EU and UK, the application is called a Marketing Authorisation Application (MAA) and covers both small molecule and biologic products.

There is a globally harmonised application process to market new drugs, which specifies all the data that must be submitted for evalution of a new drug. This is known as the electonic Common Technical Document.

The Common Technical Document (Electronic)

The eCTD is the template that must be used to submit a licence application to market a new drug. Licenses are required initially for a company to run trials in humans, following successful safety testing.

It is not mandatory for a CTS to use the eCTD for IND/CTA applications. It is for the Regulatory Authority to specify the information it requires for their evaluation.

For an application to market a drug, however, submission of an eCTD is mandatory. As mentioned previously, the websites hosted by the competent authority responsible for any particular country or economic area, should be your first port of call, otherwise important changes could be missed.

An internet search on *'electonic technical document'* will provide more details if required.

Common Technical Document (Electronic)

The three compulsory modules are shown below:

- Module 3: Chemistry (aka Quality)
- Module 4: Nonclinical Study reports
- Module 5: Clinical Study Reports.

The sections above the modules provide overviews and summaries.

Module 3 is titled 'Chemistry'. This is short for 'chemistry, manufacturing, and controls' (CMC, alternatively termed Quality).

The CMC section of the dossier is where all the details about suppliers, manufacturers, material and product specifications, test procedures, etc must be declared. To gain approval from FDA, the production facilities making the active pharmaceutical ingredient (API) and drug product (DP) must undergo a thorough physical inspection by suitably qualified inspectors. These normally require four days on site, after which an inspection report is written. A successful inspection leads to a green light for the company. Deficiencies can lead to failure and severe issues for the NDA or BLA applicant.

FDA terms these *pre-approval inspections (PAIs)*. PAIs are an essential supply chain safety net aimed at preventing defective drugs being approved and marketed in contravention of pharmaceutical law.

It is crucially important to recognise that drug safety is determined by the nonclinical Module's 3 and 4 in combination. That is because safety tests must be carried out on the material that will be administered to patients. It has never been acceptable to regulatory authorities for a clinical trial sponsor or product license holder to merely test a trial batch(es) for safety and infer all future production will be safe. The way that is assured is by these companies adhering to good practices (GxP), covered in the next section.

Module 4 is titled 'Safety'. As well as assuring the drug is not toxic to the human body, it is also important to understand what the body will do to the drug as it is broken down. Readers may be less familiar with the latter concept—that while the drug aims help a disease, the body may do something to the drug compound that may convert it into a form which could cause harm over the short or long term.

This is where Drug Metabolism and Pharmacokinetics (DMPK) comes in. The main areas to test are:

- How the drug is absorbed.
- Where it is distributed in the body.
- How the body transforms (metabolizes) the drug.
- How quickly/by what route drug/metabolites are eliminated from the body.

Readers wishing more depth on the topic can refer to Metabolism and Pharmacokinetic Studies on the FDA website.

Module 5

If preclinical safety testing is successful (typically takes 3 years), the next stage is to run clinical trials to study the drug in humans. In the US, the application is known as an Investigational New Drug (IND). The company submitting the application is known as a Clinical Trial Sponsor (CTS).

Supply Chain Regulations And Good Practices

Regulations lay down good practices (GxP) that pharmaceutical companies must comply with. They are the law and are listed below:

- Good Laboratory Practice (GLP)

- Good Clinical Practice (GCP)
- Good Manufacturing Practice (GMP)
- Good Distribution Practice (GDP)

The role of the regulatory authority is to license and inspect companies and organizations to ensure compliance.

All four apply across the supply chain in certain areas. The predominant ones relating to the supply chain are GMP and GDP.

In the EU, GMP and GDP have been combined in recent years to form GMDP. This reflects the growing importance of transport, storage, and distribution in the pharmaceutical industry.

The Regulations are published as Rules and Guidance for Pharmaceutical Manufacturers and Distributors.

In the US, there are some differences. GMP is termed current Good Manufacturing Practice (cGMP) and there are no specific regulations titled GDP. cGMP is included in the US Code of Federal Regulations (CFR). FDA's portion of the CFR is in Title 21, which interprets the Federal Food, Drug and Cosmetic Act and related statutes, including the Public Health Service Act.

The main elements of cGMP are:

- 21 CFR Part 210: cGMP in Manufacturing Processing, packing, or Holding of Drugs:

- 21 CFR Part 211: cGMP for Finished Pharmaceuticals.

- 21 CFR Part 600: cGMP Biological Products: General.

FDA is known to rely on The United States Pharmacopeial Convention (USP) document titled USP <1079> for distribution standards.

There is an amount of regulatory flexibility when it comes to standards in the supply chain for producing preclinical test material, given the early stage of development.

For trials in humans, however, production in the supply chain intended for use in humans must comply with GMDP in the EU and cGMP/USP <1079> in the US.

Before a compound can be administered to humans it must be cleared for use in humans by both animal studies and in vitro (test tube) assessments. Initial toxicity studies are designed to determine a safe starting dose in humans. The toxicity testing bar is raised as human clinical trials progress.

This comes under the heading of nonclinical testing. Nonclinical means it includes safety testing pre-clinic and the manufacturing supply chain which produces the compound for testing.

Readers wishing more depth on the safety can refer to Drug Safety Information – FDA's Communication to the Public on the FDA website.
...and so it goes.

The typical length, from beginning to receipt of the product in the pharmacy is 2 - 3 years. That is what is known as the cumulative lead-time. It means that the companies at the beginning (raw material producers) are producing materials for drugs that will be needed in 2 or 3 years' time.

The quantities they produce depend on projections, estimates, and forecasts. These are handed down from the companies along the chain. The company developing or selling the drugs at the top of the chain must start the ball rolling, based on sales expectations in their business plans.

When a seismic change in demand occurs, as with COVID-19, it is going to severely challenge the best of supply chains. When the supply chains have been neg

CHAPTER 3
PHARMACEUTICAL
SUPPLY CHAINS

O nce produced and approved for sale, both small molecule and biologic drugs share the same distribution channel to market. Figure 1 shows a simple diagram.

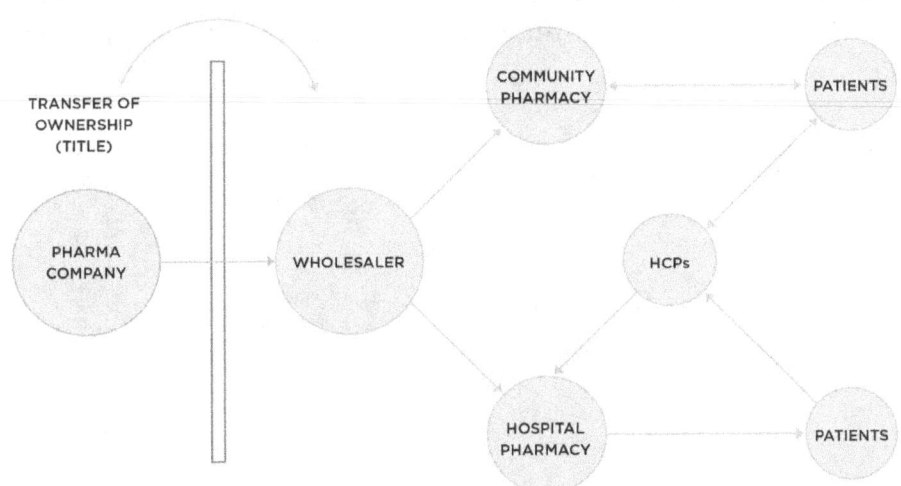

Figure 1. Stages in the distribution supply-chain for small and large-molecule (biologic) products

Both small-molecule and biologic products move through the distribution supply-chain. The wholesaler stores and moves finished products to pharmacies to be available for patient use.

Wholesalers are regulated in the same way manufacturers are, under Good Distribution Practice regulations (EU), or equivalent in countries outside the EU/UK.

Wholesalers buy the products from the companies holding the marketing authorisations (aka product licenses).

From that point onwards, the license holders are no longer involved in the physical distribution, although they still have responsibility for pharmacovigilance (collecting reports of adverse events and acting on them where relevant).

Production Supply Chains

Figure 2. shows the stages involved in producing a small molecule drug. Some stages may be combined within the same facility. For example, intermediates may be produced as part of producing API.

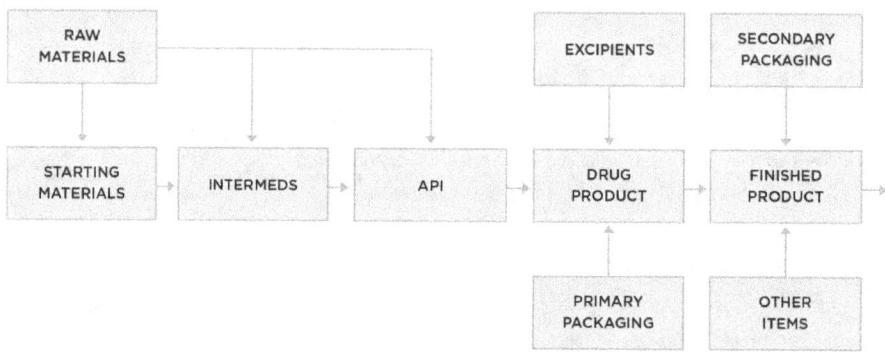

Figure 2. Stages in the production supply chain for small molecule products.

Starting Materials are materials that will form a significant part of the molecular compound when it is finished.

That means its quality must comply with the requirements of

GMP and GDP. The term API represents Active Pharmaceutical Ingredient. It can also be referred to as Drug Substance (DS), especially in the United States.

Drug Product (DP) is the dosage form (eg tablet, capsule, sterile injectable).

To produce the dosage form (DP), DS is mixed with non-active ingredients. These are commonly known as excipients. Excipients help the manufacture of the dosage form and the performance of the drug in the body.

The important points to know about small-molecule drugs are the following:

They are relatively stable at room temperature (c. 20°C). That means during storage they degrade slowly over time. The shelf-life is therefore long, typically in the region of two to five years.

The manufacturing processes involved are defined by specifications. and testing the manufactured products to make sure they meet specifications.

That means different companies, using different plant and equipment, can produce nearly identical products so long as they use the same route of synthesis. That means they use the same steps in processing the product. They must also to work to GMP and GDP.

Transferring the manufacturing technology between production plants is a well-defined series of activities known as 'technology transfer'.

Technology transfer of small-molecule products is regarded as straight-forward when carried out by suitably qualified staff.

Small molecule drugs have historically been 'one-size-fits-all'. The only thing that varies is the amount of drug in the dosage form (eg tablet or capsule) or the quantity in the pack. Supply-chain logistics is therefore comparatively straight-forward.

Biologics Supply Chains

Figure 3 shows the stages involved in producing a biologic product.

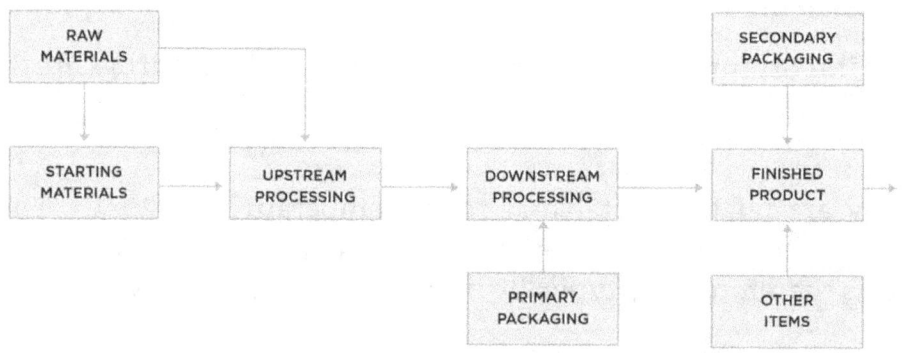

Figure 3. Stages in the production supply-chain for biologic (large-molecule) products.

Starting Materials are required, as before. They are typically animal or human cells of some kind. The next stage is 'upstream processing'.

Upstream processing refers to where the process where biomolecules are grown, usually by bacterial or mammalian cell lines, in bioreactors. When they reach the desired density, they are harvested and moved to downstream processing.

The purpose of downstream processing is to isolate, purify and concentrate the drug substance (DS) received from upstream processing. Included as well is filling into the final dosage form such as a vial or ampoule. Under normal circumstances, where the finished product can be stored in a refrigerator, labelling and packaging of individual vials is part of downstream processing.

It is important to remember that biologics are an order of magnitude more challenging to produce than small molecule products. These can be reproduced reasonably accurately, independent of the facility and equipment used to make it.

In biologics, the molecules are so large and complex that it is often impossible to define their molecular structures by analysis. All that is known is that a particular process has produced something that has a particular biological effect on a patient. Other manufacturers may not be able to replicate that product and its clinical effect, even if the process appears to be the same. That has led to the industry mantra for biologics supply chains that "the process IS the product."

This has major implications for the regulation of biological products, as different manufacturers (contract or in-house) produce products that are clinically different. Only if studies are carried out to prove different manufacturers produce products that are 'interchangeable', can one be substituted for the other.

Biologics are also inherently less stable at room temperatures than small-molecule products. The sensitivity of biologics to temperature variation and other environmental factors (remember they are living things) is immense.

The exact temperature range products and materials must be stored and transported at needs to be established, registered, and maintained throughout their lifecycles. Temperature data loggers are used to monitor temperatures throughout storage and transportation, in real time.

Excursions outside a given range, say +2°C to +8°C, must be investigated and corrective and preventative action (CAPA) action taken. This is a legal requirement.

Input materials can also be problematic. They can dramatically affect yield, potency, and quality of output, as the strength (titre) of each new supply of materials can vary widely, depending on factors that are not always obvious to the acquiring company.

Obtaining accurate upstream pedigree information from suppliers, especially when the upstream supply chain leads to seemingly anonymous donors, can be a nightmare and sometimes even impossible.

Finally, the substantial costs associated with production of a biologic, given all the complications, can often kill-off what appeared to be a promising compound.

Considering all the above, biosimilars (copies of innovator biologic drugs) have been much slower to capture market share than small molecule generics.

Advanced Therapy Medicinal Product Supply Chains

A new generation of therapies have emerged in recent years – advanced therapy medicinal products (ATMPs). ATMPs are biologic in nature, the term covering cell therapy, gene therapy and tissue engineering.

These use the body's own healing mechanisms and often target conditions associated with a patient's genetic make-up. The potential to cure disease is phenomenal but it is still in its infancy; almost all the clinical trial work going on is early stage, involving small numbers of patients in the hospital setting.

There is also a sub-set of ATMPs, autologous therapies, which are specific to an individual patient. This is where the patient's own cells are extracted, modified in some curative way, and then reintroduced into the patient's body. This produces a highly challenging circular supply chain, as show in Figure 4. below.

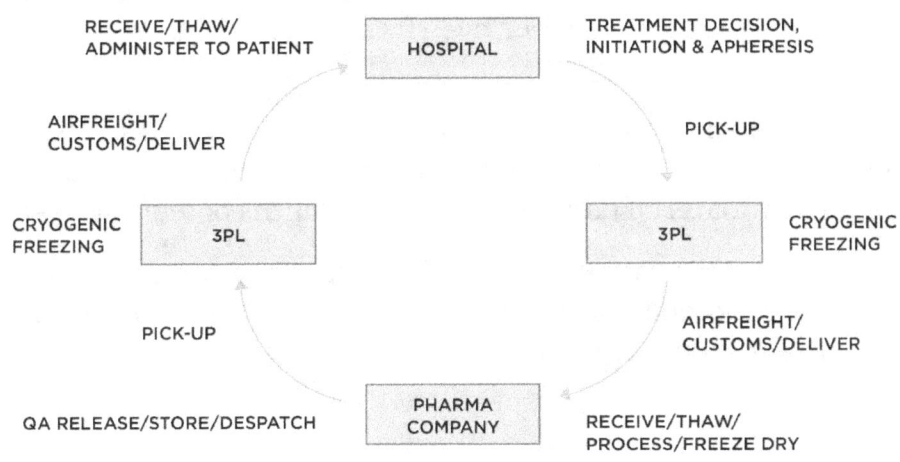

Figure 4. Supply Chain for autologous (CAR T) product.

The leading therapy area in autologous ATMPs is CAR-T, a treatment for blood cancers. First-to-market was Novartis' Kymriah, launched August 2017.

It wouldn't be an exaggeration to suggest that autologous supply chains are the world's most challenging, for the following reasons:

* The patient is in a hospital bed and the manufacturer must receive, process, and return their cells to the hospital with zero risk of compromise.

* The manufacturer must be able to produce to a batch size of a single unit.

* Shelf-life is measured in hours or days, rather than months and years, as with small molecule products.

* ATMPs are extremely sensitive to manufacturing change. A minor variation in the process can alter the product's safety and efficacy profile, placing patients at risk through unintended and undetectable variation in potency.

* The mantra for biologics, 'the process IS the product', applies

to ATMPs. Different producers may not be able to replicate that product and its clinical effect, even if the process appears to be the same.

* ATMPs can become adulterated by a second's loss of concentration. A moment's failure in concentration, from an operator or material handler, can mean months of work wasted.

* Input materials can also be problematic. They can dramatically affect yield, potency, and quality of output, as the strength (titre) of each new supply of materials can vary widely.

CHAPTER 4 MANAGING TEMPERATURE SENSITIVE SUPPLY CHAINS

A ll drugs are sensitive to temperature variation to some extent. In practice, the major focus in the industry has been on biologics. This is because living things can only survive at temperatures nature intended them to survive at. There is great variation on what those temperatures are.

With the growth of biologics coming initially from monoclonal antibodies (eg Herceptin), the service providers competing in the industry have grown exponentially, as have the temperature ranges to be serviced.

The main temperature ranges for storage are:

*   Controlled Room Temperature (CRT): +15 to +25°C.

*   Refrigerated: +2 to +8°C.

*   Freezer: -20 to -40°C.

*   Ultra-Low Freezer: -70 to -93°C.

*   Cryogenic Freezer (LN2): -190°C. and below.

Stability Data

Drug stability data must be generated to ensure product performance is retained over the intended shelf life of the product. This is known as stability testing.

The standards for stability testing required are laid out in ICH Q1A (R2) Stability testing of new drug substances and drug products.

For small molecule drugs, stability is far less of an issue than for biologics. Small molecule drugs tend to remain stable over many years, with a typical shelf-life being in the range 2 to 5 years.

Growth Of Cold Chain Management Skills

It is with the growth of biologics that the skills of managing temperature variation (cold chain management) have risen to prominence. Today, it is a flourishing industry, with many companies offering a huge range of packaging and temperature monitoring solutions.

Readers wishing to find out more on this whole area, I would recommend reference to the signposting site *Cold Chain Platform*, at:

https://www.coldchainplatform.com/

CHAPTER 5 SUPPLY CHAIN COMPLEXITY

T o give readers an idea of how complex all pharmaceutical supply chains are today, below is a list of the main actors from beginning to end:

- Product license holders
- Clinical trial sponsors
- Contract development/manufacturing orgs.
- Contract research orgs.
- Freight Forwarders, Specialist Pharma 3PLs
- Express couriers
- Integrators
- Cargo handlers, sea, air and road
- Airlines
- Shipping lines
- Wholesalers
- Pre-wholesalers
- Compounders
- Specials manufacturers
- Specialty Pharmacy Providers (SPPs)
- Community & hospital Pharmacies
- Central laboratories
- National border control

How is that for complexity!

Things can go wrong at any point, either within a manufacturing facility or during transportation from A to B.

Some Working Principles

I have developed a set of principles for managing this complexity, listed below (included in my 2017 article for Clinical Trials Arena, titled Managing the Biopharmaceutical Supply Chain: Nailing the Fundamentals).

Principle #1 – The end-to-end supply chain is the exclusive responsibility of the product license holder or clinical trial sponsor.

Principle #2 – Supply chain begins at the point where material is produced for pre-clinical testing or any other testing that will form part of a regulatory submission.

Principle #3 – A SINGLE, over-arching quality management system (QMS) should be established by the license holder or clinical trial sponsor, at the start of building the supply chain.

Principle #4 – The QMS is the vehicle by which the supply chain architecture, management reach and business processes are determined and implemented.

Principle #5 – The product license holder or clinical trial sponsor MUST define the roles for it and all the actors in the end-to-end supply chain.

Implementation

In implementing these principles, the product license holder or clinical trial sponsor should take care to:

- Understand their obligations to the license.

- Map the end-to-end supply chain by product.

- Think supply chain from early-stage development.

- Build strong relationships with service providers.

- Employ a single and effective quality system.

- Treat written agreements as 'working documents'.

- Incentivise supply chain actors to improve.

From the viewpoint of the service provider, they should take care to:

- Understand and comply with agreements.

- Confirm position in the chain of custody.

- Clarify information required from the client.

- Help define the 'process' of working together.

- Integrate with the over-arching QMS.

- Seek 'good' customers.

- Be open to gain sharing if offered.

CHAPTER 6 PRODUCT DEVELOPMENT AND SUPPLY CHAINS

I n most industries, supply chains are created as part of new product development program. The developers work together, consulting product end-users, producers, and distributors to ensure the physical supply chain they put together can deliver what is required by consumers.

For reasons we shall go into later, pharmaceutical new product development does not follow the customary approach of other industries. Rather than beginning with a consumers and working backwards from their needs, the process begins with a patented compound and moves forwards.
This results in supply chains 'evolving' with the passage of time, rather being designed and planned with the consumer in mind.

This is how it works, taking the most straight forward example of small molecule products.

The 'R' of R&D (Discovery Research) discovers (or finds) molecules using advanced technologies such as molecular modelling. Once the patent has been secured, promising compounds are handed to 'D' (Development). Development is a completely new team of specialists responsible for building a supply chain for pre-clinical testing initially. That means proving the test compound that will be produced by the supply chain is safe to study in humans.

Supply Chain For Preclinical Testing

For small molecule products, around 5 – 10 kilograms of compound will to be produced.

Figure 5 shows a typical small molecule supply chain:

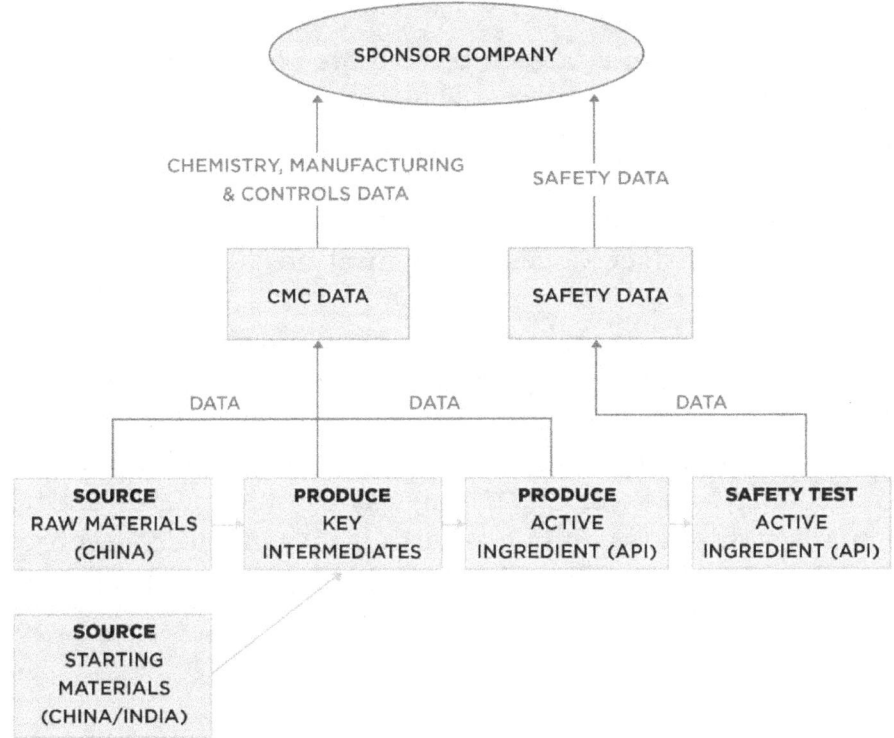

Figure 5. Small molecule supply chain for safety testing.

The production process is devised by a 'route scout' (process chemist).

Their job is to convert a laboratory process that had only ever produced small gram quantities, into a process that can yield much larger quantities. The skill involved is about making the process as efficient and 'manufacturable' as possible. A small-scale pilot plant is normally used at this stage, as the volume is not sufficient to justify occupation of commercial-scale plant.

Figure 5 shows the production of the active pharmaceutical ingredient (API). Sources of raw and starting materials will be selected by the scientists working on the project.

In this case, there are intermediate chemicals involved. Intermediate stages are not always needed; it depends on the chosen route of synthesis.

Once produced, the API is transported for safety testing at one or more chosen Contract Research Organisations (CROs).

Even though this appears to be a simple supply chain, there is already an array of suppliers and service providers involved, often spanning the globe. Remember, raw, starting materials and intermediates are sourced primarily from China and India, so ex-Asian countries are working a long way from home. For Western companies, this puts a limit on due diligence in selecting sources, and oversight when selected sites are in operation. It also adds significantly to lead-time and complexity.

Moving Forward

If it looks like the results support moving to studies in humans, the company will fill out and submit an IND/CTA. These must include all the details about the supply chain and safety data.

If approved by the Regulatory Authority, the company will be awarded a license to run trials in humans for the drug and the company is designated a clinical trial sponsor (CTS).

The CTS will plan to produce product for the first stage of clinical trials - Phase I studies in healthy volunteers.

In Figure 6, we see the extension of the supply-chain stages into production of the dosage form (eg. tablet, capsule or sterile injectable) and clinical trial kits, to be shipped into temporary storage awaiting call-off from investigator sites (hospitals and clinics).

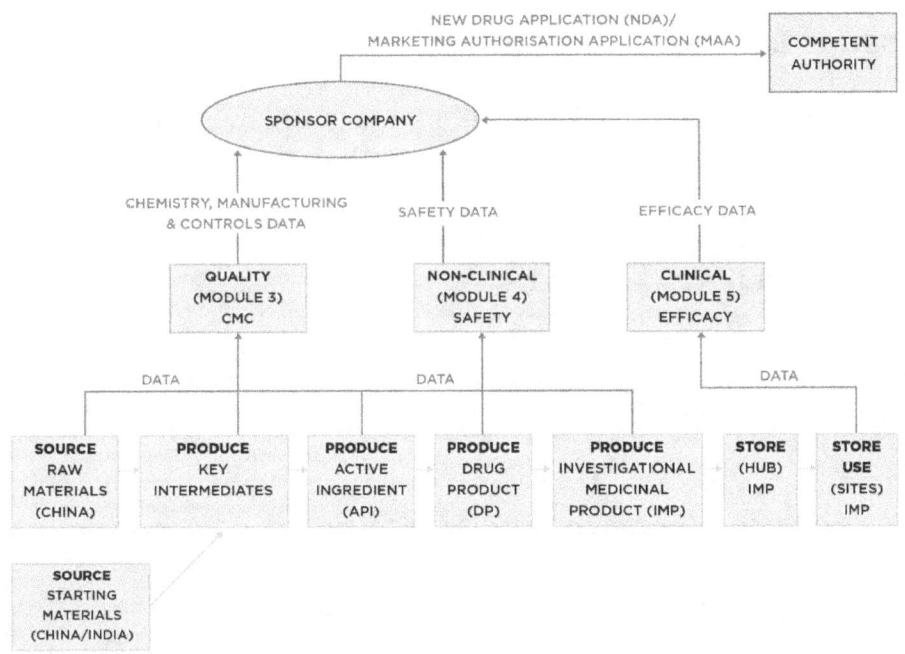

Figure 6. Clinical supply chain for trial in humans.

Each additional stage is likely to be situated in different parts of the world, with different suppliers and contractors, each with their own Quality Management System (QMS).

Submitting Module 3 Data For Launch

As the programme moves through Phase 2 and 3 clinical trials, there are likely to be a number of manufacturing scale ups to meet clinical trial demand and produce stocks for launch.

At each scale up, safety testing on the manufactured material must be repeated by the CTS, to ensure no changes have occured to the end material, such as a molecular change known as a polymorph. These can turn a previously safe material into a toxic one.

Issues Locked-In At Launch

Invariably, collection of clinical data is the primary focus, rather than building a robust supply chain. When Module 3 is eventually submitted to the Regulatory Authority, there are, without fail, serious issues locked-in that should be fixed, but can't be due to time constraints.

Here are some of the problems that will have been locked-in during development:

- Scarce/bespoke materials specified.
- Sole sourcing from far off countries.
- Inappropriate dosage form selected.
- Contractors with insufficient capacity or capability.
- Poor process yields.
- Weak compliance with Agreements.
- Analytical testing methods not accurate.
- Improper shipping/storage conditions
- Incorrect value declarations to customs.
- Weak, hands length contractor relationships

The logistical complexity and widely devolved responsibility for supply chain activities leaves those responsible for management of the supply chain with a hopeless task. In focussing on data collection and regulatory submission through the development process, the principles of professional supply chain management have been omitted. It is as if the prime purpose of a supply chain – to deliver fit-for-purpose products and services to customers – has been overlooked.

Yet the supply chain must be managed in all respects by the CTS, marketing authorisation holder (MAH), or Product License Holder (PLH).

Hopefully, readers will appreciate from the above that the issues we see in the pharmaceutical supply chains of today have their seeds in product development, where little or no strategic supply-chain management methods and principles are applied.

So, Is There Light At The End Of The Tunnel?

With my consulting hat on, there seems to be little awareness among actors in the development process of the seminal impact decisions taken here can have on the quality, cost, and service performance of the future commercial supply chain. Focus is exclusively on producing the data required to gain regulatory approval.

I never cease to be amazed at the complexity of development supply chains when they are mapped out. It is hard to find any kind of logic or strategy driving decision-making.

For example, modern-day thinking is that companies benefit from working closely with their suppliers of key components and materials. This is especially the case when there are multiple production stages to be carried out. I see little evidence of that happening in big pharma.

The final and most significant observation is this. Once the supply chain data (shown in red in Figure 7) are submitted to the Regulatory Authority for review, nothing can change before launch. That means material and process specifications, test methods, suppliers, producers, service providers, or anything else, are locked in. It is imperative to get it right before the filing goes in.

There is no practical option to change anything for product launch once the filing has been submitted. Unless the commercial supply chain requirement had been considered and acted upon before submission, it's all written in stone.

The almost infinite permutations for the physical flow of materials and products has become a major issue, where opportunites for bad actors to operate in the shadows between one genuine actor and another are rife, as we shall go on to discover.

CHAPTER 7 THE POTENTIAL FOR PATIENT HARM

I t is not just obstacles and issues locked into the commercial supply chain at launch. There is potential for a far more serious outcome.

In 2007/8, pharmaceutical supply chains became the subject of global debate among key stakeholders, but for the wrong reasons.

A tragic event occurred that shocked the world into realizing that pharmaceutical supply chains had the potential to kill and maim unsuspecting patients.

A blood thinning agent, heparin, had been adulterated due to the product license holder (Baxter) procuring a toxic substance that had been illegally substituted for the genuine registered material. The adulterated product was found to have caused nine patient deaths and 574 serious adverse events (SAEs).

The full account of this has been documented in the report: After Heparin: Protecting Consumers from the Risks of Substandard and Counterfeit Drugs, authored by PEW Health Group

This is the PEW HEALTH GROUP summary:

"In late 2007, US health officials began receiving reports of unexpected allergic-type reactions in patients undergoing dialysis. The reactions were linked to a widely used blood thinner—heparin—and specifically to an adulterant that had been introduced during manufacture of the drug in China.

The US Food and Drug Administration (FDA) believes the adulteration of heparin was an economically motivated act—a clear breach of the US pharmaceutical supply chain.

"Pharmaceutical manufacturers and distributors work together in a robust system to deliver high-quality products, but drug manufacturing and distribution have become increasingly complex in recent years. Prescription and over-the-counter (OTC) medications originate in factories all over the world, moving into the American marketplace through supply chains that can involve numerous processing plants, manufacturers, suppliers, brokers, packagers, and distributors.

"The number of drug products made outside of the United States doubled from 2001 to 2008, according to FDA estimates.

The FDA estimates that up to 40 percent of finished drugs used by US patients are manufactured abroad, and 80 percent of active ingredients and bulk chemicals used in US drugs come from foreign countries.

Increasingly, the United States relies on drug manufacturing in developing countries—mainly China and India. Globalization, increased outsourcing of manufacturing, the complexity of pharmaceutical distribution, and the existence of criminal actors willing to capitalize on supply chain weaknesses has created the potential for counterfeit or substandard medicines to enter the system and reach patients.

As evidenced by the adulteration of heparin and other case studies outlined in this report, these rare but potentially serious events can have grave consequences."

The United States President Wades In

Product shortages in the supply chain can harm patients in need of life saving drugs, according to the US President.

On October 31, 2011, President Barack Obama signed an executive order directing the Food and Drug Administration to take action to reduce prescription-drug shortages, which the White House said had endangered patients and led to price gouging. He explained the reason for the order.

"Recently, we have seen how the potential of drug shortages for vital drugs, including some cancers, can really have an adverse impact on patients and those who are caring for patients. Sometimes we run out of or run low on certain types of drugs, and that drives up prices and it increases patient risk," President Obama said at the signing in the Oval Office.

The executive order instructs the FDA to take action in three areas: broaden reporting of potential drug shortages, expedite regulatory reviews that can help prevent shortages, and examine whether potential shortages have led to illegal price gouging."

"Over the last five years, the number of these drug shortages has nearly tripled. Even though the FDA has prevented an actual crisis, this is one of those slow rolling problems that could end up resulting in disaster for patients and health-care facilities all across the country. Congress has been trying since February to do something about this. It has not yet been able to get it done, and it is the belief of this administration…that we can't wait for action on the Hill. We've got to go ahead and move forward."

Some Examples

No person, organisation or company is being singled out here. It just so happens that when I presented at and cochaired the FDA/ Xavier Health Global Outsourcing Conference from 2010 to 13, these were hot topics of debate:

"J&J/McNeil placed under a 'Consent Decree' after numerous recalls associated with supply chain issues."

"Abbott hit by $4m diagnostics theft in USA" (June 2011)
"Eli Lilly warehouse thieves make off with $76m haul" (March 2011)

"In Singapore, 150 people were admitted to hospital in the first five months of 2008 having severe hypoglycaemia – a sharp drop in blood-sugar levels. Four of them died and seven suffered severe brain damage. They had reportedly taken counterfeit copies of drugs purporting to treat erectile dysfunction, but which contained a hefty dose of glyburide, used for treating diabetes."

"Operation Singapore, largest counterfeit operation in EU, where 2 million doses of counterfeit medicine enter UK supply chain in 2006/7". The UK MHRA's 'Operation Singapore' investigation into the infiltration of counterfeit medicine into the UK's supply chain during five months in 2007 has concluded with a British man being sentenced to eight years imprisonment.

These are examples – readers may wish to do their own research on the topic.

What Was The Response From Stakeholders?

Governments, Regulatory Authorities and other concerned stakeholders collaborated globally to raise standards in supply chains for medicines and healthcare products.

In the European Union (EU) the Falsified Medicines Directive was passed in 2011, with major changes to Good Manufacturing and Distribution practice (GMDP) introduced.

In the US, the Drug Quality and Security Act 2013 and the Drug Supply Chain Security Act 2017 were passed.

Legislation Hasn't Worked

In spite of the legislation, forward (track) and reverse (trace) traceability is virtually non-existent. With so many actors in the supply chain, all with their own business interests to protect, it has become an impossible task.

CHAPTER 8 REAL WORLD EXAMPLE

In my work both as a previous permanent employee in the industry, and as a consultant, I'm typically called in to assess the maturity of a small molecule or biologic supply chain. This involves mapping the supply chain 'as is' and comparing it on where the company needs to be to achieve its target. That target always relates to the chances of the company gaining approval based on its Module 3 (CMC) data.

Believe me, the block diagrams we have relied on up to here do not do justice to the complexity of the supply chain for launch, so I am going to an example of real-world preparations for product launch, once the development work is nearing completion.

This was a project I worked on as a permanent employee in 2003/4. My role was to head up the supply chain launch activities for producing a compound to be distributed by the marketing partner. The partner was a large biologics producer based in South San Francisco.

I was brought in to bring commercial supply chain management skills to proceedings.

The marketing partner was experienced and demanding.
My employer, the company developing the compound, was on its first product launch.

It's important to say at the start that the development team were exceptionally qualified to undertake pharmaceutical development activities. The majority had worked at major pharmaceutical companies in similar roles.

The principle I'm aiming to bring out here is this. No matter how good the team is, a flawed system will result in flawed outcomes. It's the system of production on trial here.

Time To Explore The Flaws Created By The System.

There were two contractos qualified to supply API, one in Italy and one procured through a broker, based in the US.

The API contained two starting materials, each of which had three suppliers. So, now we have eight suppliers to manage, and a confusing number of permutations for potential contents of the API.

Between the eight of them, source locations included Japan, Italy, US and India. There were also brokers involved as intermediaries in the commercial procurement activites.

This was all in place before I joined—an example of an industry mantra well beyond its sell by date—never run out of API!

Can you see the issue here? If not, this is it. By allowing the supply chain to evolve according to the rate of progress in manufacture (or not), timelines slip. Once the deadline to submit the eCTD approaches, it is a race to onboard the rest of the supply chain partners, and they were losing the race spectacularly.

When I arrived, there was only one producer (contractor) of the drug product. A second source was planned, but time had ebbed away.

The sole producer had realized they were going to be in an exceptionally strong position leading up to product launch and beyond. There was no finished product packager in place at all.

There was only just enough time left before launch to complete the supply chain. Even though it was complete for launch, dosage form production and finished product packing were sole sourced. You might imagine the impact that had on purchase price.

If you can't imagine, I'll help you out. The purchase price of tablets increased 10-fold once the supplier's lawyers realized there was no alternative source. That was not the worst of it, given the supply chain risk of failure with sole source arrangements.

There were other issues locked-in that would severely restrict the performance of the commercial supply chain.

In pharmaceutical supply chains however, that does not get much executive management attention. Having product in the pipeline to sell is the primary C-Suite concern.

Was It Always Like This?

Actually no, it was nothing like this before blockbusters came along.

During my years at Bayer in the UK from 1980 to 1996, raw materials and ingredients arrived in the goods receiving bay from sister and EU-based companies. They were processed, made into dosage forms, and packaged as finished products to be sent on their way to the hospitals and pharmacies around the UK.

Non-UK markets were mainly handled by shipping to other Bayer legal entities around the globe. Those Bayer entities had local presence and distribution capabilities in their own home markets.

Links with customers were direct, and the staff at Bayer, the company holding the license to sell the products, could handle customer complaints.

The staff in the Bridgend plant, making Alka Seltzer for the EU, had a standing joke. A polystyrene packing piece was at the top of each glass bottle as a cushion to prevent the tablets from moving and breaking.

It was a frequent occurrence for customers to send the piece back to the plant with a complaint that it wouldn't dissolve. The reply was always polite and understanding, but staff found it hard to resist a wry smile.

Figure 7. shows how it was in those days:

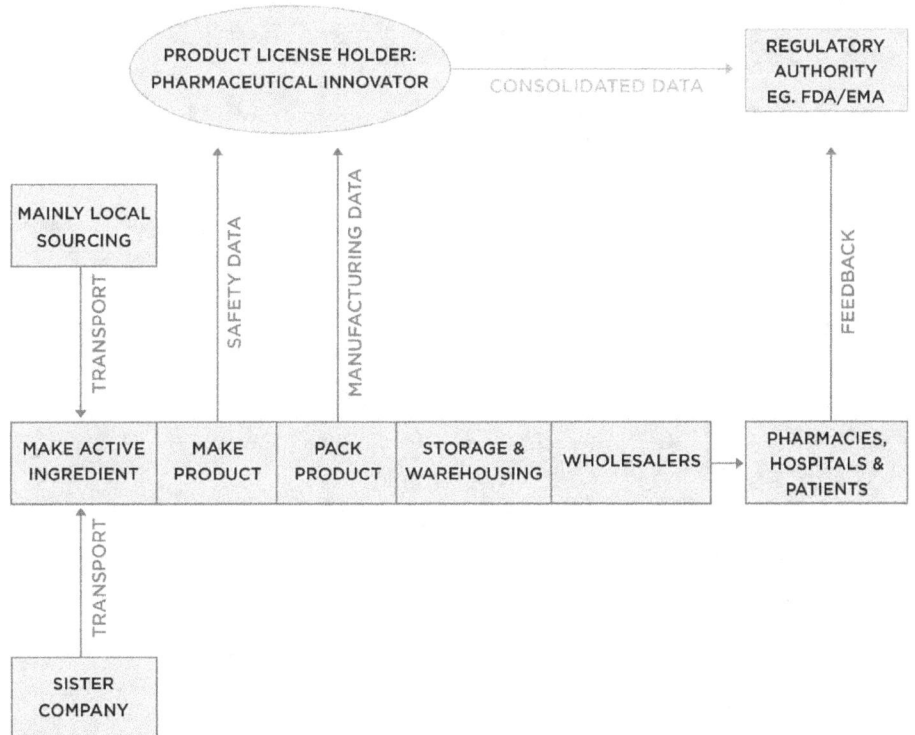

Figure 7. Vertical Integration Pre-Blockbusters.

That was life before the blockbuster era. It was an era when companies knew that developing and 'producing' drugs was crucial to converting promising ideas in the laboratory into drugs to be administered to patients.

Even more crucial was the realization that it's the manufactured and distributed product that goes into a patient's body, not a promising idea.

CHAPTER 9 HOW DID IT GET TO THIS?

I n 1976, the pharmaceutical company Smith, Kline & French (SK&F) launched Tagamet (cimetidine), an anti-ulcer treatment. The head of the program, Sir James Black, was the first to employ rational drug design in practice, bringing Tagamet to market over twelve years of intense research and development activity.

Five years after the launch of Tagamet, Glaxo launched a competitive product, Zantac (ranitidine), based on a similar compound but produced by a cleaner manufacturing process.

Within five years, Zantac was outselling Tagamet 3:1.

This was the first example of clever targeting of physicians to capture competitor markets. It stimulated phenomenal growth in the therapeutic area. Both products became blockbusters on sales of tens of billions of dollars. The beginning of a lucrative strategy for the industry was cast.

Glaxo's Formula Gets The Thumbs Up.

Other prmaceutical companies and their Investors were impressed by what Glaxo had achieved. Even the CEO of SK&F congratulated them on their win.

Armed with this apparently powerful strategic model, pharmaceutical companies resolved to beef up sales & marketing, awaiting compounds coming down the pipe. Discovery research grew like topsy, as great libraries of patented molecules were required to feed the hungry marketing machine.

Expert statisticians and medics were hired to help the marketers frame the messages to doctors. Regulatory affairs departments were expanded to be sure of keeping on the right side of the regulators.

So, the scene was set. Sales & marketing, with their supporting cast, were poised ready for the next blockbuster compound to come down the pipe. Discovery research was out there, plotting theories on why a molecule would work, modelling and patenting them in great quantities and stuffing prime suspects into the upstream end of the pipe.

In the investor community, however, there was emerging realization that not much was actually making its way out of the pipe. The prospect of being lumbered with huge fixed costs if a drug failed was a serious concern.

Coincidentally, during the '80s, other sectors were outsourcing 'non-core activities', claiming significant benefits in risk reduction, plus lower costs to boot. That seemed like the perfect solution.

Discovery research and marketing were considered core activities. The bits in the middle, running clinical trials, producing, testing, moving, and storing products and materials, dealing with customers using the products, were all classed as non-core...

...and so the cull began.

The exact sequence of events isn't easy to pin down, but the results were unmistakable—masses of workers were shown the door and non-core facilities went up for sale.

Ousted senior executives looking for pastures new put the assets to good use. They set up small companies (SDDs, small drug developers) developing drugs to either sell to Big Pharma or try to get to market themselves.

The CEOs in SDDs were making a persuasive case to be the engine room of drug development, citing less bureaucracy and shorter chains of command. Venture capital (VC) investors liked the sound of it, and started funnelling cash in.

Meanwhile, other exiting senior executives joined together and bought up the facilities, funded by a different cadre of investors – private equity.

The companies formed provided SDDs with pharmaceutical development services in exchange for a fee, under contract. One set of service providers became known as contract manufacturing organisations (CMOs). As the scope of their work extended into product development, some of the larger companies were called contract development and manufacturing organisations (CDMOs).

Another set of executive exiles formed contract research organisations (CROs), offering clinical development services, such as clinical trial monitoring, data management and safety testing.

Many of the rest of the redundant staff became consultants. Not the McKinsey kind, more former employees selling their skills back into the industry under contracts of varying length. I became one of them myself.

Also on the agenda was the tricky business of supplying hospitals and pharmacies. Handling customer complaints and dealing with ever more frequent deliveries were not deemed core and Big Pharma handed over all of its warehousing and distribution assets to gratefully receiving wholesalers.

Similarly, specialist third party logistics providers (3PLs) grew their businesses helping with the burgeoning volumes of materials and products that needed to be stored and transported around the ever-growing supply-chain.

The final arm of the strategy was what I've dubbed 'out-throwing'; the practice of dropping existing products once the patent expired, as they didn't meet ROI targets the branded versions had enjoyed.

Up sprung companies with more modest profit aspirations working to much tighter margins, copying the originals. This gave rise to the generics industry, where, at last, competition was going to save the day, or was it?

How Did The Dynamic Pan Out?

The number of SDDs began to accelerate as the potential rewards in doing a licensing deal with a large pharmaceuticals company were immense. These new boys on the block were developing drugs themselves, hoping to eventually hand the baton on to bigger players.

There was similar growth in the size and number of CDMOs and CROs, since business was brisk, as both the SDDs and pharmaceutical companies increasingly needed their services.

The Drug Price Competition and Patent Term Restoration Act of 1984 ("the Hatch-Waxman Act") gave a welcome boost to the use of generics and this, in turn, was more business for the CDMs and CRO's.

With the growth of biologics, more companies entered the fray. Biosimilars, the generic equivalent in biologics, were attempting to capture innovator markets as patent expiry loomed. Again, they needed the services of CDMOs and CROs.

The ever-increasing availability of services to cover almost every aspect of drug development encouraged universities to 'spin out' their research ideas into SDDs on the trail of pharmaceutical company attention and licensing deals.

Government grants and funding bodies were set-up to support progress. All this time, the contractors had been consolidating, supported by private equity, who regarded service providers as high potential, less risky investments...

...and all was not rosy in the pharmaceutical company garden.

When Was There A Whiff Of Things Going Awry?

The first piece of definitive evidence of problems emerged in 2006. The United States Government Accountability Office (US GAO) issued a report, GAO-07-49, titled *NEW DRUG DEVELOPMENT: Science, Business, Regulatory, and Intellectual Property Issues Cited as Hampering Drug Development Efforts*, in November 2006.

Amongst other things, it showed a chart of the failure rates and timelines during the development of a drug.

Figure 8. below show a diagram reproduced from the GAO Report:

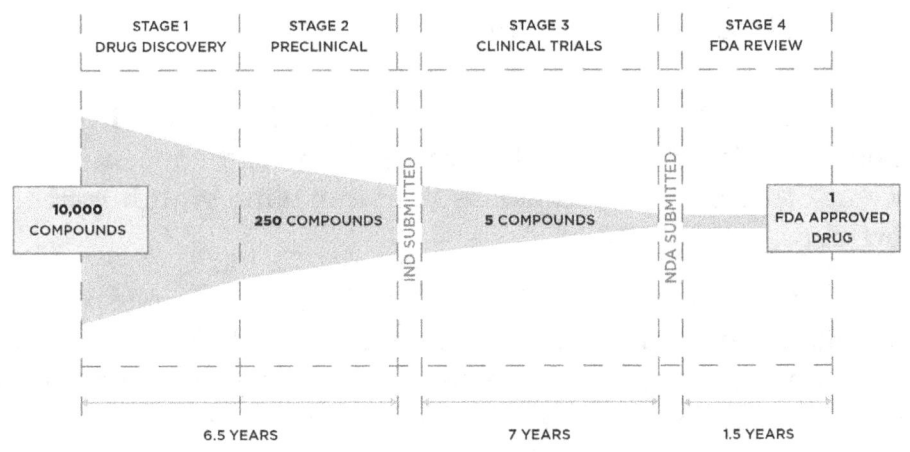

Figure 8. Failure Rates and Timelines in Drug Development

The statistics:

* 10,000 screened molecules from the patent portfolio.

* 250 reach preclinical testing.

* 5 enter clinical trials.

* 1 approved for sale.

Timelines:

Preclinical phase = approximately 3.5 years

Clinical phase = 7years

NDA submission to approval = 1.5 years

That is 12 years in total.

In 2012, Joseph A. DiMasi, PhD, of Tuft's University, presented at the Pharma Integrates Conference in 2012. He confirmed the US GAO figures above, suggesting things had got worse since then, quoting five out of six failures in clinical trials.

Pharmaceutical Companies Press On Regardless As Service Providers Thrive.

Pharmaceutical companies have continued to retrench into opposite ends of the drug lifecycle so they can concentrate on buying other pharma companies (horizontal integration) or their portfolios.

That leaves most of the work of testing, developing, making, storing, moving, and distributing drugs to third parties. Not that those third parties (service providers) are not capable of providing good or even excellent service. Just their priorities are with their owners to make profits for themselves and their investors. They therefore have no skin in the game nor any contact with customers.

The service providers have continued to grow like topsy.

CROs have become big, powerful providers of clinical and non-clinical services through consolidation.

Consolidation has also taken place in the CDMO world, and specialist third-party logistics providers (3PLs) have also been part of the consolidation and growth.

The finished product distributors of pharmaceutical products are now mega corporations, on the back of consolidation. In the US, three companies own around 90% of the distribution channel.

The three-company ownership was similar in the EU, until a few years ago, where the US corporations began gobbling up EU-based wholesalers.

The generics industry has grown enormously on the back of payer demands for cheaper drugs. Up to 90% of drugs now sold in the US and UK are generic. Ironically, in later times, the intense competition for out-of-patent drugs has subsided, which has led to spiralling rises in generic drug prices.

This again has been attributed to M&A activity leading to far less, bigger players on the field being able to pick and choose what they supply. The ever-present shortages have added weight to the hikes.

So, the valley of death, as it became known, was swallowing up most of the compounds entering development. It was commonplace to read of drugs failing in phase III trials, where the hopes and dreams of patients were dashed.

By way of example, there have been over 30 late-stage clinical trial failures in Alzheimer's over the last 15 or so years. Millions of animals culled, with little or no contribution to medical science. Billions of dollars poured down the drain.

That's The Sickening Cost Of A Failed Strategy.

In response to the valley of death swallowing up compounds, pharma companies began to employ several tactics to maintain revenues from the declining pipeline of blockbusters.

Health Economics and Outcomes Research (HEOR) became a new tool in the box. The idea behind it was to develop arguments to justify the asking price for new drugs. Market access groups were formed to put the HEOR arguments in front of payers, as a starting point for negotiation.

Markets also targeted were perceived less challenging regulatory environments and patient populations.

These include rare diseases, orphan indications and treatments for cancer. The unfortunate side-effect was that prices had to be astronomic because of the very small sales volumes involved.

Mergers and acquisitions carried on at pace, but nothing was done to deal with the underlying problem massive failure rates in drug development.

An Entire Industry Fooled

That's the nub of it then—an entire industry fooled into thinking easy money was on the way. Glaxo's success with Zantac inadvertently created an illusion that even surprised itself.

As an 'accidental illusionist', Glaxo did what magicians do. It deflected audience eyes away from the hand enabling the magic (SK&F), onto the hand performing the show. The illusion was met with thunderous applause, as it unfolded before their eyes. The audience left, filled with the potential of repeating the magic for themselves - $ signs were spinning in investor eyes.

In the real world, the illusion can be explained using the lifecycle of a drug shown in Figure 9 below:

Figure 9. Lifecycle of a pharmaceutical patent

There were, and still are, three key milestone dates—patent award, regulatory approval, and expiration of the patent. Then two broad phases—product development and market exploitation.

Glaxo's success with Zantac turned eyes towards the period between approval and expiry, the market exploitation phase (red line), and then leftwards to the all-important patent award.

Pharmaceutical companies looked toward the blue line of product development and could only see routine drudge, cost drain and risk exposure. It apparently seemed reasonable to jettison much of product development out of the boat and leave it to others. The real 'science' was perceived to be a numbers game in discovery, where serendipity played a leading role.

Zantac had taken just five years to get to market and with the technology breakthroughs in molecular modeling and other computational techniques. The thinking then was that finding promising molecules could only become easier over time.

This shone a spotlight onto remaining patent life, the time available to wring the market. Consciously or unconsciously, pharmaceutical heads turned towards the thing that was eating up the remaining life—product development.

Developers' behavior reflected the heat heading their way. No-one wanted to be caught mouthing "wait a minute; I'm not ready to move on". The mantra handed down was "every day's delay is $2M in lost sales". This became a useful stick to beat people with, metaphorically, of course.

Any developer raising a red flag on the suitability of a molecule for the clinic and market risked a slapped wrist, so they didn't say anything and got on with their jobs.

Once a molecule entered the pipe, there was no way back. No time for any iterative dialogue between discoverers and developers, looking at alternatives if issues were found. The discoverers were off to other searches for compounds with blockbuster potential, sorry; I mean drugs to treat patients with unmet medical needs.

The First Dagger In The Heart

This was the first dagger into the heart of pharma was playing the numbers game, hoping for the best. Placing its compound chips on the table of regulatory roulette. It seemed one big blockbuster win would more than compensate for all the losses.

The Second Dagger

The second element of the unfortunate strategy was outsourcing the people skills and facilities that were crucial to their ability to develop new drugs.

Pharmaceutical companies had not anticipated the pitfalls of inappropriate outsourcing of critical assets. Here is a world leading expert on the topic of procurement and outsourcing, Professor Andrew Cox, to tell us more. This was his summary of the situation:

All of these recent developments lead to a serious questioning of the strategic outsourcing undertaken by the major pharmaceutical companies in the recent past. Not only has there been an inadvertent loss of critical assets, but also an increase in competition and a loss of control of key suppliers and supply chains.

Unfortunately, this has occurred at a time when competition from generic companies has increased and when profits from patented products have been in decline. The result has been an industry experiencing widespread decline in profitability, now responding with short-term knee-jerk merger and acquisition strategies. This is a telling indictment of the failure of strategic outsourcing in the pharmaceutical industry.

These are powerful words from the professor and should send a chill through the hearts of industry executives and investors.

For reinforcement, there is also a fairly recent example of failure to outsource effectively in the aviation industry - Boeing's excursion into outsourcing of product development for the Dreamliner.

Boeing was attempting to do the same as Pharma, which was to "shift the economic risk onto [their] suppliers."

Previously, Boeing had "maintained tight control over the design" and provided detailed specifications to suppliers. The telling comment is "by outsourcing the design and the manufacturing, Boeing lost control of the development process." Boeing eventually recovered by choking back their outsourced model, but not without major issues of delays and overspend.

Pharma was not so lucky. It has fallen into all the pits and discovered a few more besides!

Dagger Three Finishes It Off

The final killer strike was passing drug development onto small drug developers (SDDs). This was a direct result of outsourcing. In the development of any product, crucial decisions are made at the outset that can have a huge impact on the success of the undertaking. It is commonly estimated that 80% of cost and risk is locked-in during the development process. In pharmaceuticals, given the difficulty of changing due to regulatory constraints, it is even higher.

SDDs did not, and never will, have the critical mass to build the necessary foundations for a commercialize-able supply chain.

As an example, think of an aircraft manufacturer being approached by a small group of scientists. They say they have a revolutionary new design of plane on its way to market—they've made some wings and bolted a propeller and lawnmower engine to them. No-one died in testing during early trials.

The scientists ask the manufacturer if they would like to buy it to go the rest of the way to market. What would you say if you were the manufacturer?

That may be an extreme analogy, but hopefully you get the gist. Pharmaceutical products must be produced in the same way an aircraft, aeroengine or silicon chip has to be.

The Real Magic

The hand performing the real magic was SK&F's development effort in bringing Tagamet to market.

In 1964, SK&F set up an acid secretion program in its UK arm, with a vastly experienced team from across the drug development disciplines. They were pioneers of rational drug design, whereby a drug was designed based on knowledge of a biological target known as a receptor. This contrasted with the industry tradition of trial-and-error testing according to the serendipity principle.

Over the pond at SK&F was another set of gifted individuals developing the PROCESS to make the drug as a commercial proposition. This in-company collaboration was reported to have worked incredibly well.

One account, by the American Chemistry Society (ACS) commented on the development effort, "[This] is a story of single-minded commitment by a group of creative scientists working in close collaboration in the United Kingdom. The process of research and development for economical production of the resulting drug, cimetidine [Tagamet], was the work of equally creative scientists working in the United States."

The head of the cimetidine (Tagamet) program, Sir James Black, later received the Nobel Prize for his drug research.

Sir David Jack, who was responsible for Glaxo's development effort in bringing Zantac to market in only 5 years, was quoted as saying: "The development of Zantac had not been in the same order of inspired breakthrough as the research which produced Tagamet... It's not necessary to shake the earth on its axis to make money in this industry. We simply improved on James Black's product by choosing a substance with a cleaner reaction."

So, here is the illusion laid bare.

The real success was the fully integrated drug development effort WITHIN THE SAME COMPANY. A patent was awarded for the PROCESS at commercial scale, not a few grams of compound in a test tube.

CHAPTER 10 BACK TO THE FUTURE FOR PHARMA

What we now know is that pharmaceutical companies took a wrong fork in the road in the 1980s. Instead of following SK&Fs example of the hard yards of drug development, it took the easier, more lucrative alternative.

In fact, the Zantac experience put an end to a drug development era. Prior to that, physicians, doctors and healthcare professionals were at the heart of drug development, as we will go on the explore.

Penicillin

The penicillin story is well known. For those that need reminding, the mother of all antibiotics was developed by Alexander Fleming. On his return from holiday in August 1928, he noticed that bacteria had not grown in one of his culture dishes. He obtained an extract from the mold in the dish, naming it 'penicillium'. The rest is history...or is it? Not according to Robert P. Gaynes, author of Germ Theory, and the article The Discovery of Penicillin – New Insights After More Than 75 Years of Clinical Use.

In his book, Gaynes states "Due to its importance in medicine, the story of penicillin's discovery has become shrouded in legend and distorted truths." Gaynes' article explains the distorted truths, summarized below. Fleming did not have the wherewithal to properly identify the mold strain or make it in any quantity.

It took a team at Oxford University, headed by a gentleman named Howard Florey, to purify enough penicillin to run pre-clinical (1939) and clinical (1941) studies. They were a great success, but they didn't know how to make sufficient quantities to supply the market. In 1941, Florey and a fungal expert, Norman Heatley, visited the USA to mull over the problem.

The scenario was put to a microbiologist named Andrew J Moyer, an expert in the manufacture of molds, working at the United States Department of Agriculture Northern Regional Research Laboratory in Peoria, Illinois. Moyer and his team came up with the idea to "culture the penicillin in a mixture of corn steep liquor and lactose, thereby greatly increasing the yields and production rate". Moyer applied for a patent in May 1945, which was awarded 3 years later.

So why did the myth persist?

An article in The Times reported the breakthrough in Oxford but failed to mention Fleming or Florey. Fleming's boss wrote to The Times, extolling his virtues and Fleming talked freely to the press at the time. Florey didn't say a dicky bird to the press.

So, the real account of it was never told. In a nutshell, the story goes like this. Fleming discovered strong evidence penicillium was killing bacteria but was not able to isolate or purify the active ingredient. Florey's team in Oxford isolated and purified enough to make test quantities, which produced even more evidence, but they were not able to manufacture it in more than low gram quantities. A J Moyer's team devised the commercial process and supply-chain to make penicillin in exponentially greater quantities and he was awarded the patent.

This led to successful mass production of penicillin to satisfy the demands of the World War II. The article comments,

"Unprecedented United States/Great Britain cooperation for penicillin production was incredibly successful." Moyer applied for a patent of the manufacturing process in 1945, which was granted in 1948. The paper explains "The Fleming Myth" was down to an article in The Times following an interview with Fleming, but Florey and his staff refused to comment.

This myth therefore perpetuated and has become hard coded into the industry psyche. This has created a public illusion that drugs are 'discovered' through serendipitous findings.

Nothing could be further from the truth. The important takeaway is there were 11 lost years while Fleming was looking for someone to help him identify what was active in the mould. He eventually hooked up with Oxford University in 1939. By early 1943, the US Government had entered World War II and facilitated the transfer of Moyer's process to Merck and other large pharmaceutical companies.

Just imagine if Fleming, Florey, and Moyer had been collaborating in August 1928, when the discovery was made – potentially, four years to get such a ground-breaking compound to market! There are more examples of the power of collaboration in the days prior to the blockbuster era

Insulin

In 1921, on a shoestring budget at the University of Toronto, several young scientists began investigating a possible treatment for Type 1 diabetes. They found that by grinding up and purifying animal pancreases, and then regularly injecting the material, they could treat Type 1 diabetes in dogs.

After first testing the drug for safety by injecting themselves, the scientists treated a 14-year-old boy with Type 1 diabetes. His recovery was almost miraculous, going from death's door to good health in a matter of weeks. By 1923, the scientists had won the Nobel prize and the treatment had entered mass production in collaboration with Eli Lilly and Company and the Swedish organisation Nordisk. The scientists patented the drug and sold it to the University of Toronto for three dollars (one dollar for each researcher), thinking that this was the best way to ensure that affordable treatment would be available to everyone who needed it.

With a fast forward to the future, fast-acting 'analog' insulins were pioneered with Lilly's Humalog in 1996, but when Novo Nordisk entered the market four years later with its own analog insulin, NovoLog, prices did not decrease due to competition. Instead, Lilly and Nordisk followed each other closely in an exponential price increase. When Humalog was first introduced, it cost $21. At the time of writing, HumaLog costs [$295.35] per vial and NovoLog costs [$296.27]. The older 'human' insulins like Humalin are less expensive, but far less effective in treating Type 1 diabetes — yet even these primitive insulins have increased dramatically in price since their introduction in 1982.

The HPR article: 'How insulin became unaffordable' recounted the tragic case of Alec Raeshawn Smith, whose body stopped producing insulin when he was 24 – he had become a Type 1 diabetic. The article goes on: "For two years, Smith managed his condition relatively well. But it wasn't easy financially. On May 20, 2017, Smith turned 26, ageing out of his parents' insurance." He didn't qualify for government assistance with his insulin payments, and when he went to pick up his insulin in early June, the bill was over $1300 without insurance.

He couldn't afford the medicine that day and decided to ration his remaining insulin until he was paid. He didn't tell his family. On June 25, Smith went to dinner with his girlfriend, where he complained about stomach pains. It was the last time anyone saw him alive. He called in sick to work the next day. On June 27, Smith was found dead in his apartment. RIP Alec Raeshawn Smith: our hearts go out to his mother, Nicole Smith-Holt, his family, and all those who knew and loved him.

Polio Vaccine

The first effective polio vaccine was developed in 1952 by Jonas Salk and a team at the University of Pittsburgh. Salk went on CBS radio to report a successful test on a small group of adults and children on 26 March 1953; two days later the results were published.

Beginning 23 February 1954, the vaccine was tested at Arsenal Elementary School and the Watson Home for Children in Pittsburgh, Pennsylvania.

On April 12, 1955, Edward R. Murrow asked Jonas Salk who owned the patent to the polio vaccine. "Well, the people, I would say," Salk responded. "There is no patent. Could you patent the sun?"

By the time of his chat with Murrow, which aired on the day, the polio vaccine was announced as safe and 90 percent effective, Salk was already more messiah than virologist to the average American. Polio paralysed between 13,000 and 20,000 children annually in the last pre-vaccine years, and Salk was the face of the inoculation initiative. Appearing on television to present the vaccine as a gift to the American people was a public relations masterstroke.

One critic of Big Pharma called Salk "the foster parent of children around the world, with no thought of the money he could make by withholding the vaccine from the children of the poor."

There are three important takeaways from the above.

Firstly, if Fleming, Florey's team and Moyer's team had been together when that initial discovery was made, it would have taken less than 4 years from start to finish, instead of the 15 years it actually took – cutting the time to market to one quarter of what it actually took.

Secondly, Fleming was a physician as well as being a microbiologist. As a healthcare professional, he was looking for new medicines that could cure conditions he was very familiar with in his day-to-day work.

Sir Frederick Banting, famous for his work to isolate insulin in the early 1920s, was similarly qualified as a physician, as was Edward Jenner, who brought the smallpox vaccine to the world.

Jonas Salk, who famously refused to patent his polio vaccine, was a virologist who choose to do medical research instead of becoming a practicing physician. He was, never-the-less, a medical expert in the disease, carrying out the development work personally along with his team.

The final takeaway from penicillin, and from each of the medical breakthroughs above, is the degree of evidence that was assembled on the safety, efficacy and manufacturability of the compound PRIOR to moving into a working supply-chain.

They effectively created prototypes before exposing any more than handfuls of patients to the medicine. Some even tested for safety on themselves when confidence levels were sufficiently high.

It should not surprise you to learn that Sir James Black was also a physician.

The move to focusing on discovery research to find patented molecules changed all that. Physicians had to move aside to let the scientists take over the show.

CHAPTER 11
MEDICINES FOR THE
21ST CENTURY

I hope to have convinced you that the dysfunction in pharmaceutical supply chains can be traced upstream to drug development, driven by the race to exploit patents. Also, that wholesale change is the only way forward.

To add a broader spectrum of opinions to our study, let's return to some of the inputs collected during the conference mentioned earlier, *Medicines for the 21st Century: Safe, Better, Cheaper*.

Inputs On Issues And Opportunities

Inputs on issues and opportunities were categorised, post-conference, under seven headings, shown below, along with a brief summary of inputs made:

• Patient and HCP relationship – should be closer, with a more even 'partnership' relationship developed (in relation to sharing of information on medicines prescribed). Healthcare professionals (HCPs) do not have direct access to information on the drugs they prescribe from those companies holding licences to market them. Neither do actors in the distribution network, once ownership transfers to them from the manufacturing or finished goods site of storage utilised by the licence holder.

• Screening and prevention – there is an over-reliance on intervention with medicines, in place of focus on prevention and screening. Observed also that pharmaceutical companies concentrate on prescription medicines (and the associated supra-profits) at the expense of screening and diagnostic products. Given diagnosis and therapy go hand-in-hand, especially in an era of precision medicine, the question arises how are pharmaceutical companies
going to be encouraged to adopt more balanced investment strategies?

• New product development (NPD) – lack of 'design thinking' that is focused on end-users of medicines, with insufficient investment from pharmaceutical companies in early-stage product development. Large pharmaceutical companies have become extremely risk-averse and have adopted strategies to transfer risk into the supply base, with a subsequent loss of control. We ask the question, if pharmaceutical companies base their new product investment decisions on calculations of the net present value (NPV) returns, who is going to invest in less lucrative therapeutic areas and diagnostics?

• Supply-chain integrity – lack of control and integrity due to overly complex, outsourced supply chains. Legislation has been passed, both in the EU (Falsified Medicines Directive 2011 - FMD), and US (Drug Supply Chain
Security Act - DSCSA), to help ensure the industry can track and trace its products from finished goods manufacturer to patient, in an attempt to address issues of counterfeiting and economically motivated adulteration. We ask why does it require Governments to legislate on supply-chain controls, when the companies holding responsibility for them do not tackle this issue head-on, as part of their obligations to supply chain integrity?

• Intellectual Property Rights (IPR) – the patent system is not seen as being balanced with respect to risk and reward. In the industry today, it is incredibly easy to gain a patent award, based on very little actual evidence of it being able to convert into a commercial proposition. In contrast, the rewards associated with regulatory approval of an NME (New Molecular Entity), can amount to tens of billions of pounds over in-patent life. There are international initiatives on-going at the moment which the UK is not currently involved with.

• Education – medicines are a major healthcare intervention yet there is very little quality knowledge and education taught in schools and other centres of learning, about the 'dos and don'ts' of medicine. If progress is to be made in improving relationships between HCPs and patients, patients need a basic understanding of the risks and benefits associated with medicines and how to ask the right questions of their HCPs. Topics could be what medicines cost, how they're produced, the importance of taking them correctly, and the impact when patients don't do so, both on their health and the data that then
impacts on the production of that drug.

• Transparency - publishing negative results, as well as the positive, in biomedical science, and reducing wastage of repeating the same useless results/experiments, is seen as a priority; also, it was noted that promotions and press releases relating to positive results of clinical trials were not helpful to objectivity in clinical trials. It was noted that the opioid crisis in the US, again, has its roots in lack of transparency in operations of the companies concerned.

Our Conclusions

We believe, by consensus, that our prima facie starting hypothesis has been validated and we conclude that the medicines system of today is not fit-for-purpose; or broken. We reached that conclusion as a group, based on the evidence around us and the research we were able to carry out.

So, what is the extent of that 'broken-ness'?

We suggest it is far greater than you might think. It was fortunate that Ray Perkins PhD was able to travel from Kentucky to join us on the day of the conference, to share with us his deep understanding of the history and science of medicines discovery and development.
Dr Perkins is an acknowledged expert and kindly provided an account of how and where the system is broken. This is a summary:

o The application of medicine is broken - the ability to select medicines for patients presenting with symptoms is worse than hit-or-miss

o In 2018 in the United Kingdom, one billion prescriptions were written - 900 million of those did nothing.

o Nine of ten patients are exposed to side effects, some worse than the disease itself.

o Biological research is broken - it is now universally recognized – by scientists and institutions alike – that a minimum of 50% of published findings cannot be reproduced.

o Within the context of this document, it must be acknowledged that the foundational "knowledge" for development of new medicines and diagnostics is likewise corrupt.

o The Genes-are-Destiny model is broken. It is recognised now humans are composite creatures and must be approached as such.

o One of the first scientists to sequence the human genome recognised the limitations of using genes to predict and prevent

disease: "We simply don't have enough genes for this idea of biological determinism to work."
(Craig Venter, Chairman and CEO of J. Craig Venter Institute).

o The failure of genes-are-destiny must be seen in contrast to its inverse: biology must be approached at the functional level of complex, interacting networks of molecules, cells, tissues, organs, organisms and the environment.

What should we conclude from this?

In simple terms, studying genes, genetics, and other human biology is not going to get medicines to patients.

If we take penicillin as an example, we do not know what the mechanism of action is, all that's known is that it's safe, works, and can be manufactured at scale. It took blood, sweat, and tears from doctors, chemists, manufacturing experts, and many others to do the job.

It's the same for any other drug.

The Downward Spiral

The downward spiral began in the early 1980s, as the large pharmaceutical companies (Big Pharma) began to employ a strategy that has negatively impacted their ability to develop and supply safe, differentiated medicines at affordable prices. The strategy involved retaining the activities of discovery research and sales & marketing in-house, while outsourcing to third parties the work of testing, developing, manufacturing, storing, moving and
distributing medicines.

The root causal issue is identified as pharmaceutical companies manipulating patent law following the beginning of the blockbuster era. The development of new medicines has increasingly become a game of chance, as thousands of molecular compounds are 'discovered', patented and defended, in the hope one compound gets through. Before the blockbuster era, patents were not awarded until the establishment of a successful manufacturing process for patient supply (eg penicillin, Tagamet, Zantac; the polio vaccine were never patented).

This has resulted in the following:

o A dis-integration of the R&D function, as discovery research works in isolation from development. Compounds entering development from discovery research cannot be re-evaluated and replaced in the light of new or unexpected findings.

o The crucial link between end-users of medicines and pharmaceutical companies developing them, has been broken. The pharma companies sell their products into the distribution channel, for third parties (wholesalers)
to deal with patients, hospitals and pharmacies. There is no meaningful two-way communication link.

o Critical assets and competencies required to develop differentiated products have been lost to the supply base.

o Without these critical assets and competencies, the power and control has transferred from the buyer (the pharmaceutical company) to the seller (the service provider). This has been described by world leading exponent of strategic procurement and supply, Professor Andrew Cox as 'unforeseen post-contractual moral hazard'.

o Now in a considerably weaker position compared with the pre-blockbuster era, pharma companies are unable to drive down costs, initiate quality improvement programmes or extract additional value for money from the supply/value chain.

Outsourcing

We note that Boeing experimented with this strategy with the Dreamliner and subsequently had to revert to a more orthodox development model. This extract from the article *Why Boeing's Dreamliner was a nightmare waiting to happen* explains:

The technological leap was always likely to cause teething issues. But these were exacerbated by Boeing's decision to massively increase the percentage of parts it sourced from outside contractors. The wing tips were made in Korea, the cabin lighting in Germany, cargo doors in Sweden, escape slides in New Jersey, landing gear in France.

The plan backfired. Outsourcing parts led to three years of delays. Parts didn't fit together properly. Shims used to bridge small parts were not attached correctly. Many aircraft had to have their tails extensively reworked. The company ended up buying some suppliers, to take their business back in house.

We suggest here that Pharma companies have not adjusted their outsourcing strategies as Boeing had to; in fact, the practice is continuing apace. The conclusion is, therefore, that similar issues of cost over-run, delays and lack of a coordinated approach persist in the pharma industry, albeit it is not readily observable to an untrained eye.

Then we asked ourselves the question *"How does inappropriate outsourcing negatively affect any product development activity?"*

Our conclusion is that there is a fundamental difference in terms of quality of communication and responsiveness between in-house resources, compared with resources owned by third party organisations.

Where there are multiple outsourced relationships across the value chain, complexity and miscommunication is significantly amplified.

Additionally, commitment by employees in third party organisations is to the contract that has been signed with the company awarding the contract.
There is only an indirect link with the success of the product, and if there is a conflict, adhering to the contract is the priority, so that their company objectives are not compromised. This is not a criticism of the quality of the services these companies provide, rather it is a business reality.

We therefore conclude that there should be a reversal of the degree of outsourcing that has taken place in the industry, such that the large pharmaceutical companies re-purchase some of the organisations they have previously divested.

Drug Development Outsourced Too

Issues are not limited to outsourcing of the physical conversion activities of medicines development and supply.

The earlier stages of the development process have also been outsourced to smaller companies, which we have earlier termed SDDs.

This suffers from a similar problem of ownership, in that their objective is to sell their work onto Big Pharma companies. SDDs do not have the critical mass to fund and undertake the necessary foundational product development practices that would reduce the probability of failure and enhance the product performance once on the market.

Discontinuing Out Of Patent Products

Aside from outsourcing, we observe also the negative impact of large pharmaceutical companies discontinuing supply once their products are out-of-patent.

With a typical in-patent life eight to ten years, the opportunity exists to drive down costs according to the learning curve effect, so that healthy profits can still be made from the product. We should be aware that the generic companies that take over do not have that advantage nor the benefit of being the sole source provider.

The advent of generics companies has added huge complexity to the industry, with no apparent benefit to patients that could not be delivered by the originator company.

At Least A Generation Of Change

Given that this dynamic has been operating for over 40 years, there will be at least a generation of change required to reverse the spiral of declining performance.

We look towards the examples of penicillin and Tagamet which were models of collaboration, and conclude the system should return to the principles and practices of those days, yet harness all the advances that have taken place in predictive technologies over those years, which are being pursued in our universities but still to be harnessed by pharmaceutical companies.

CHAPTER 12 DRUG DEVELOPMENT FOR THE 21ST CENTURY

A new paradigm is required, and it isn't even new. It's about learning from the past to lay a path for the future.

The previous chapter tells us how successful physicians, doctors, and other healthcare professionals (known collectively as HCPs) were at working in collaboration with experienced partners to develop drugs. So, the first strand of drug development for the 21st century is engaging deeply and meaningfully with HCPs.

The next strand is to move from the current three step process of discovery, development, and production, to just two-steps—prototyping and production.

Prototyping is used in almost every other industry, except pharmaceuticals. In aviation, it is wind tunnels and flight simulators, using the full weight of STEM – Science, Technology, Engineering and Mathematics.

At the core of STEM is integration of all the skills required to bring products to market. 'TEM' is the missing ingredient we want to put back in the pot. So, with a mix of learning from the earlier takeaways and knowledge of modern-day production systems, the following approach is suggested as a starting point.

* Include all the required disciplines at the beginning (penicillin suggests it could reduce time-to-market to one quarter of what it is today).

* Co-develop with a representative number of healthcare professionals (HCPs) with deep knowledge of the indication (disease state) PRIOR to pre-clinical work.

* Construct a Voice of End-user (VoE - patient and HCP).

* Consider diagnosis and therapy together – precision medicine demands it.

* Integrate 'discovery research' and 'development' into a single group. Call the group DESIGN.

* DESIGN develops small-scale prototypes, tested for safety, efficacy, and manufacturability by relevant disciplines. Make maximum use of ex vivo methods (e.g. organ-on-a-chip, testing in tissue).

* Prototype in the hospital setting, with the necessary resources in situ.

* A single group will hold responsibility for preclinical, clinical, and commercial supply chains. The group will use 21st century principles and practices to design, manage and improve the supply chain.

* This group will have advanced skills equivalent to those brought to the West following the Japanese revolution in production systems.

A Production System Approach To Drugs

The automotive industry in the Western world may have felt fortunate when it was in a similar but less-extreme position around sixty years ago. In those days, the automotive industry was producing one-size-fits-all products that end users either liked or lumped. It was working to a formula that had delivered the goods for many years, placing customers toward the back of the line.

Then the Japanese production system revolutionized the industry. Toyota's leader, Taiichi Ohno, observed a fundamental change in the market for an automotive during the 1950s.

He identified the following as the drivers for change:

- Instalment payment plans
- Used car trade-ins
- Sedan-type bodies
- Changing models yearly
- Improved roads

From that, Ohno concluded that customer markets were moving past the one-size-fits-all paradigm of the Model T Ford. Markets were becoming more segmented, and customers were increasingly seeking variety and customization. In effect, Ohno predicted the end of the "blockbuster" auto era.

The Japanese industry proved that the days of producing huge volumes to drive down unit costs, often at the expense of quality, were numbered. Customer was becoming king.

Accordingly, a new model for product development emerged. The message was to build a deep understanding of the value proposition that would capture the imagination of the end user and then build a production system to deliver on that value.

The old R&D approach, often termed 'throwing it over the wall', whereby R&D paid little attention to the needs of manufacturing and supply in their designs, was deemed inadequate in markets seeking variety and customization.

This is the model that the pharmaceutical industry has steered clear of to this day. The 'patent' cosy blanket has served it well for many a year, why change now?

It is the patent 'soother' that must be taken away, and now it is not a moment too soon to begin working on it.

CHAPTER 13
ROADMAP TO A
BETTER FUTURE

This is all well and good, I hear you think, but pharmaceutical companies are never going to change their attitude towards supply chains or anything else, are they?

Not without some help, obviously – who would willingly give up a sumptuous lifestyle?

It's not that the regulators haven't tried either.

Something readers should be aware of is that there is a long history of regulatory modernization initiatives emanating from FDA. In particular, the work of Janet Woodcock MD.

Dr Woodcock's work began in the early 2000s, with GMPs for the 21st Century.

At that time, she was Director, Center for Drug Evaluation and Research at FDA – a pivotal position.

The document (referenced above) is quite technical, so I'll lay out the principles in layman's terms here.

The initiative points towards under performance in pharmaceutical manufacturing and supply chains, and the impact that has on patients. It then points to the solution for pharmaceutical companies – to adopt the same practices that modern-day companies in other sectors utilize, especially Quality by Design (QbD) (alternatively named Design for Manufacure (DfM)).

There are two main components to the QbD proposal:

Design products so that they can be manufactured effectively and with the end user in mind, rather than had over molecular compounds for a development group to make the best of.

Use all available technology (eg Process Analytical Technology - PAT) to replace physical inspection at the end of production lines.

The reference is above and readers with a technical background may want to explore further. Otherwise, we can move on.

A few years later, the Critical Path Initiative (CPI) was launched.

In my opinion, this was a seminal document. It explains how pharmaceutical companies could use technology in drug development, such as using biomarkers to predict the efficacy of a drug. There were several other potentially game-changing proposals in there.

Of course, you can take a horse to water, but you can't make it drink; and true to form, pharmaceutical drug developers have not drunk a drop. The sumptuous lifestyle appears to still get in the way.

What Is At The Root Of This Refusal To Change?

At the root of all this is an archaic provision in chemical patent law, 'compound claims'.

This allows a company, with enough money to pay for a patent, to claim a compound as their own. They can then put it on the shelf so that no one else gets it. They don't have to prove the compound is suitable to get over the valley of death.

All they must do is explain why the compound could cure or

modify a disease. We know that in 9,999 cases out of 10,000 it doesn't get to market, let alone help with a disease.

It doesn't take a genius to work out the balance of risk and reward is out of alignment with patent awards in any other industry sectors.

For example, imagine some inventive individual, working in the automotive industry, applying to patent a molecular compound from which to make rubber that would help tyres hold the road better.

The inventor would be out on the street and told not to come back without a prototype tyre on a wheel with evidence of improved road-holding properties.

No one would see that as unfair because all the difficulties of proving the case for commercial success are still to be worked out. If the case is proven, then protection should be given as a reward for sticking with it.

That is the principle behind patents – rewarding the efforts of the inventor for the hard work in proving the product has a commercial future. The patent stops others, who have not done the work, from stealing the idea and making a profit from it.

In pharmaceuticals, the only work required to get a patent is to draw a chicken wire diagram of the molecule, write a theoretical justification of why it would modify or cure a disease, and make a trip to the bank to withdraw the necessary $$$ to pay the patent office.

Is There Any Hope For The Future?

There could be if we follow the advice of Professor Russell Ackoff, the US Systems Thinker.

His sage advice was:

*"Don't fight the system, change the rules and
the system will change itself."*

Of course, rules drive behaviour, good and bad. Gaming patent law is endemic in the industry, creating hugely profitable monoloplies.

Compound claims patent law is clearly the culprit, and I have been banging on about that for years.

That was made clear in the whitepaper that emerged from the conference mentioned earlier, titled:

MEDICINES FOR THE 21st CENTURY: *Safe, Better, Cheaper.*

I sent the white paper to the Clerk of UK Parliament's Health and Social Care Committee (HSCCOM), prior to the General Election in December 2019. The Clerk acknowledged receipt but informed me he was not allowed to circulate unsolicited papers from third parties to the Committee. He did, however, allow me to submit a one-page summary of a proposed inquiry the Committee could carry out.

I duly obliged. This is the text of it:

Suggestion that the Health and Social Care Committee should undertake an inquiry into pharmaceutical company use of patent law.

Nature of the inquiry

Pharmaceutical companies use patent law to create monopolies/ oligopolies to deliver super-normal profits, with minimum application of internal resourcesi. The reference Patients not patents recounts how this works against the interests of healthcare stakeholders in the UK, EU and indeed, global healthcare systems.

There has been a dramatic change in pharmaceutical company strategy since the early 1980's. Prior to this, patents were not sought until a feasible manufacturing process for the medicine had been established. However, subsequently, companies have been patenting molecular compounds, rather than the process of manufacture, with major consequences as outlined below.

The impact of patenting molecular compounds

This new approach has resulted in the following:

• A steady reduction in new medicines entering healthcare systems.

• Attrition rates resulting in well over 90% of medicines under development failing to gain regulatory approval.

• Increasingly frequent stalemates between payors and pharmaceutical companies over pricing and affordability (eg Vertex/Orkambi) impacting patient morbidity and mortality.

• Lack of technology uptake (esp. from UK universities) when it comes to the use of predictive methods that could replace much of animal testing.

Such an inquiry would investigate alternative innovation reward models to restore the balance of risk and reward in medicines development.

What kind of evidence would we want the Committee to collect

* NHS perspective on the extent to which healthcare professionals and patients are invited by pharmaceutical companies to contribute to and be involved in medicines development (e.g. PFMD, EUPATI)

* Regulatory (eg MHRA, EMA) input on quality and compliance issues identified across the pharmaceutical supply chain, and the

impact of outsourcing and offshoring.

* Trade association (eg ABPI, BIA) perspectives on the above and their ideas for remediation.

* Legal input on the methods used by pharmaceutical companies to secure patents?

I'd heard nothing up to the election.

After the election, I re-sent the paper and request for inquiry to Rt Hon Jeremy Hunt MP, who had taken over as the new Chair of the Committee.

To my surprise, this is email I received back:

"Dear Hedley,

Thank you for submitting the attached inquiry proposal into pharmaceutical company use of patent law. However, at this moment in time the Committee has not yet been established and therefore the Committee's future work programme remains undetermined.

As you may be aware the Committee also receives many requests for inquiries into various aspects of health policy, administration, and expenditure. It is not always possible to accommodate all of these suggestions as the Committee has the opportunity to undertake a maximum of around six to eight detailed inquiries each year.

Your proposal will be made available to the Committee, alongside other requests for inquiries which I have received. Should the Committee decide to look further into the matter, I will ensure that the Committee secretariat informs you and gives you the opportunity to make an input into our work.

Yours sincerely,

Rt Hon Jeremy Hunt MP

Chair of the Health and Social Care Committee"

That felt like a major step forward, even if there was nothing guaranteed. Then COVID-19 came along, and lockdown stopped everything.

In time, hopefully, things will return to an even keel and the Committee see fit to raise the inquiry.

The Backup Plan

If changing patent law does not get through, there is still a solution based on changing rules, a la Professor Ackoff.

The IND application to run clinical trials is the opportunity. Traditionally, the supply chain requirements at the IND stage have been less than onerous. Similarly, for non-clinical and clinical aspects. The historic rationale for this is that innovation is not stifled at such an early stage, and promising compounds get a fair chance.

The counter to that is if only one in 250 development compounds get to market, there is not a lot of innovation in there to stifle!

The suggestion is to ask pharmaceutical companies to collect more evidence of a compound's potential to deliver a safe, effective, manufacturable drug to market. This would be done at the IND stage.

Also, predictive technologies have moved on unrecognizably in the last 20 years, so why wouldn't you use it at an early stage, prior to trialing in humans?

A number of approaches to predictive technologies are outlined in the Critical Path Initiative, and surely, with a will, the industry could take them on and deliver more besides.

This would require closer engagement between HCPs and drug developers to make it work. This is because much of the clinical evidence would need interpretation by qualified medics with deep understanding of the medical condition (indication).

If this happened, they wouldn't be thinking about scaling up production, they would be intent on identifying compounds that meet agreed criteria as prototypes.

This is not an easy task, and we can't pretend it is. Like any innovation though, you have to suck it and see with safety parameters similar to aircraft design.

This is also wholly aligned with QbD, which calls for companies to design drugs that can be manufactured to meet the needs of patients. Their needs are for safe, effective, high-quality drugs.

Let's do it!

———————————————

AFTERWORD

Having got this book out, I'm delighted to say that my next book will be published by Wiley, NJ.

The editor of the first book contacted me in May 2023, having seen my Substack *Inside Pharma*, which I began writing in January 2022, asking if I was interested in writing a second book.

Cutting to the chase, I was and the contract is agreed and signed. The working title is:

Transforming the Pharmaceutical Supply Chain

The Preface is below:

PREFACE

With this book I've endeavored to bring fresh thinking and perspective to building, managing, and improving pharmaceutical supply chains. In so doing, my fervent and enduring aim is to help catalyze disruptive innovation in this globally important industry.
Although new to pharma, the approach recommended is not actually novel in any way. Nearly every other industry sector uses, at least to some degree, the principles I will outline here for you. Ultimately, businesses only survive in the long term by consistently delivering value for money to those using their products. The pharmaceutical industry has been delinquent on this score for many a year.

You may be surprised to learn that this is not my first attempt.

In 2011, *Supply Chain Management in the Drug Industry: Delivering Patient Value for Pharmaceuticals and Biologics* was published by Wiley. At the end of chapter 17, the concluding chapter, I wrote the following:

The third milestone [from *Supply Chain Management in the Drug Industry*] was to help catalyze change in this industry, and hopefully, the book has sparked a desire to contemplate a better way to develop and run pharmaceutical supply chains. In my opinion, that change can happen only when there is a massive redefinition of business models, as discussed above. This, in turn, should drive toward patient-centric supply chains founded on sound SCM [supply chain management] principles, If the third key milestone were to come to fruition, the author believes that the fourth would be an eventual outcome—those in the industry would start to realize the importance of SCM and become passionately interested in moving the profession forward.

That book had excellent reviews, but as you would expect, the established system that was the pharmaceutical industry then, just as it is today, did not heed the cautions. Changing tack to an easier to understand book, I used Amazon CreateSpace (now Amazon KDP) to self-publish a follow up book titled: *Find It, File It, Flog It: Pharma's Crippling Addiction and How to Cure it.* I resorted to giving the drug development and commercialization processes a funny name, *Find It, File It, Flog It*, and semi-ridiculing the notion of scientists discovering blockbuster drugs in the dead of night, surrounded by test tubes, Bunsen burners and other apparatus involved in deep chemistry.

The audiences were always polite. No one challenged me on what I said, although there may well have been skepticism underneath.

As it turned out, for the second time, neither the pharmaceutical industry nor the world outside of it were ready to seek out the messages.

Putting my thinking cap on again in late 2018, I decided that a conference workshop might get the messages out further and wider. This is the summary of the event:

"On May 8th, 2019, a group of clinicians, patients, representatives of relevant charities, experts in product development, legal, regulatory and supply chain specialists gathered in Wales, with the aim of examining that claim, based on facts and evidence.

The day was organised in workshop format, and the day's session was titled "MEDICINES FOR THE 21st CENTURY: Safe, Better, Cheaper". It involved in-depth dialogue and transfer of knowledge, over three panel sessions, between invited attendees and panel members, considering issues and opportunities in relation to safe medicines, better medicines, and cheaper medicines.

Proceedings over the day were recorded on video, and live polling was used to collect inputs from those in attendance."

In the white paper I collated following the conference, the suggestions below stood out like sore thumbs:

• Set up multi-disciplinary education.

• Teaching children in schools about meds, what they cost, how they're produced, the importance of taking them correctly, and the impact when patients don't do so.

• Educating patients regarding the medicines they use rather than prescribing and then the patient looking at the information slip that comes in the box.

Yes, of course, that's it!

The pharmaceutical industry was effectively a big black box and those inside were happy for it to stay that way. In counter, it seemed to me at least, that the world needed multi-level education on the fundamental principles and processes that apply to the development, manufacture, and distribution of drugs. This has, for so long, been a no-go area.

Then I thought of the words of the great Eli Goldratt—sacred cows make great steaks!

That set me on a course aimed at developing a virtual education program for university students' studying relevant degree subjects. Fortune then smiled on me, as not long after I was contacted by the careers department from the School of Applied Sciences at a university just down the road from me in Wales, the University of South Wales (USW).

It has been run as a pilot program and feedback has been received. It went down well.

Then, as if we needed reminding, the SARS-CoV-2 enigma broke. Amongst the unfolding fear and confusion, supply chain questions began to emerge from unexpected quarters, not normally associated with such matters.

Almost overnight, a new audience searching for honest answers to the conundrums they had observed sprung up. In response, at the beginning of January 2022, I started a Substack titled Inside Pharma, which was well received by subscribers.

Inside Pharma attracted the attention of the editor of my first book, who asked if I would be interested in writing a second book. If you are reading this, I was, and hopefully you find what you are looking for in what follows.

Hedley Rees, August 2023

ABOUT THE AUTHOR

Hedley Rees

Present Appointment (2005 to date):

Hedley Rees is the managing director and lead consultant at PharmaFlow Limited, a UK-based consultancy specialising in the strategic design and management of preclinical, clinical, and commercial supply chains in the pharmaceutical and life science industries.

Clients range from large pharmaceutical companies to emerging biotech, investors, lawyers, other consultancies, facility design & build specialists and third-party logistics providers (3PLs). Assignments span preclinical, clinical, and commercial supply chains up to complex multi-product networks covering global territories.

Qualifications:
B. Eng. (Tech) Hons, Production Engineering, University of Wales.
Executive MBA, Cranfield University School of Management.
Previous Appointments in senior management positions:
Bayer UK (1980 - 1996)
British Biotech (1996 – 1999)
Vernalis (1999 – 2001)
Ortho-Clinical Diagnostics (2001 – 2003)
OSI Pharmaceuticals (2003 – 2005)

Achievements and Affiliations:
Author, Supply Chain Management in the Drug Industry: Delivering Patient Value for Pharmaceuticals and Biologics, Wiley, 2011

Advisory Board Member, International Institute, Advanced Purchasing & Supply (IIAPS).

Advisory Board Member GMP Review (GMP = Good Manufacturing Practice).

Former consultant to Oxford BioMedica on UK Government funding call Advanced Manufacturing Supply Chain Initiative (AMSCI), resulting in funding award of £7.1M.

Former Advisory Board Member to Marken, 2011 - 2012 (now a UPS company).

Founding Member of Expert Industry Panel for CPhI Worldwide (UBM plc)

Former member of the UK Bio-Industry Association's (BIA) Manufacturing Advisory Committee, 2007 – 2011

Conference Speaking Engagements:
"Why patient-specific (autologous) therapies need hospitals to manufacture; and how to go about it.", National Healthcare Expo, 26th November 2019, ARENA MK, Milton Keynes.

"How Whole Systems Thinking Will Transform the Pharma Supply Chain", Making Pharmaceuticals, Coventry Ricoh Arena, April 30th, 2019.

"Building Robust Advanced Therapy Value Chains with Rapid Prototyping and Systems Thinking", Making Pharmaceuticals, Coventry Ricoh Arena, April 25th, 2018

"A practitioners view on supply chains in Pharma & Biotech"
Pharmaceutical Licensing Group (PLG), Fasken & Martineau LLP,
London, October 23, 2014

"A Provider Perspective on Building Patient-Centric Supply
Chains", UPS EU Healthcare Annual Conference, Hungarian
Academy of Science, Budapest, October 1, 2014

"De-risking the Pharma Supply Chain from Day 1..."
Jardine Lloyd Thomson (JLT) Insurance Annual Conference,
Windsor, UK May 16, 2014

"Implementing QbD like other industries – successfully!"
FDA/Xavier University PharmaLink Conference, Cincinnati,
March 13th, 2013.

"Is the Pharma Supply Chain a Lost Cause?", QUMAS CONNECT
Annual Conference, Tampa, Florida, Feb 4th, 2013.

"The Power of Integrated Supply Chains, by Design",
36th International GMP Conference, University of Georgia March
14th, 2012.

"Good Distribution Practices: What do they mean to you?"
International Society for Pharmaceutical Engineering (ISPE)
Annual Conference, San Francisco, November 14th, 2012.

"Building, Managing and Continuously Improving Clinical Supply
Chains", IQPC Clinical Trial Supply Europe, Basel, February 1st,
2012.

"The Power of Integrated Supply Chains, by Design"
FDA/Xavier University Global Outsourcing Conference,
Cincinnati, October 4th, 2011.

"Building Supply Chain Transparency and Pedigree"
FDA/Xavier University Global Outsourcing Conference, Cincinnati, June 16th, 2010.

"The Importance of Quality by Design in Biotherapeutic Development", Bioindustry Association Manufacturing Advisory Committee, London June 4th, 2009.

"Building, Managing and Continuously Improving Outsourced Value Chains in Biotech", Next Generation Pharmaceutical Summit, Evian, Lake Geneva, May 7th, 2008.

"Building, Managing and Perfecting Supply Chains in Pharmaceuticals" ManuPharma European Summit, Noordwijk aan Zee, Netherlands, 18th May2005.

Journal Article Publishers:

Chemistry Today
GMP Review
Industrial Pharmacy
Pharmaceutical Technology
Pharmaceutical Journal (PJ),
Pharmaphorum
European Biopharmaceutical Review

Background:

Hedley's skill set covers the range of competencies from strategic procurement, production and inventory control, distribution logistics, information systems and organisational improvement. His early career was spent as an industrial engineer in the automotive, consumer durables and FMCG sectors.

As an expert in production systems and industrial improvement methods, Hedley is a zealous advocate of the regulatory modernization frameworks of FDAs 21st Century Modernization and the International Council for Harmonisation of Technical Requirements for Pharmaceuticals for Human Use (ICH) Guidance's Q8 – Q12.

Hedley regularly delivers podcasts, webinars, and presentations at international conferences. He was co-chair of the highly regarded FDA/Xavier University sponsored PharmaLink Conference (formerly FDA/Xavier Global Outsourcing Conference) held in Cincinnati annually, from 2010 - 2013.

Hedley is focusing his time now on developing and delivering digital education programmes for various stakeholders in the pharmaceutical industry, believing knowledge and education is the only route to long term, sustainable resurgence for the pharmaceutical industry.

PRAISE FOR AUTHOR

37 years in the industry but I never saw the production side in this light; I have learned a lot. I will write 2 reviews, one for general audiences and one for the trial lawyers who need to read it in their efforts to remediate injuries from generic drugs that had unexpectedly adverse effects.

Using charts, graphic imagery and guest writers' insightful comments, this text delivers an excellent message for the corporate executive, the investor in pharma stocks, the regulatory professional and (last and least) the lawyers who advise the company.... Every reviewer has a list of wished-for items, but I'm pleased to say that Rees's book met all of my needs and then some.... Rees has a keen eye for what could go wrong in the drug maker's supply chain.

- JAMES O'REILLY, PROFESSOR IN FDA LAW AT THE UNIVERSITY OF CINCINNATI AND CHAIR OF THE FDA COMMITTEE OF THE AMERICAN BAR ASSOCIATION

This book is ideal reading for those entering or currently working in the field of supply chain management, such as clinical supply managers, or those in operations or production and planning ... This book would be an excellent resource for small pharmaceutical companies that may have limited experience of supply chain implementation or outsourcing, giving a thorough overview of the process and plenty of food for thought.

Hedley Rees' book is a timely antidote to the faddish advice and writing about outsourcing and lean supply chain management that has bedevilled good practice in the industry, and in supply chain management thinking in general. In a series of well researched and documented chapters about the pitfalls of inappropriate practice in the end-to-end supply chains for pharmaceuticals and drugs this volume demonstrates the key problems faced by the industry in managing supply chains holistically and for customer value. It also provides useful insights into the major positioning methodologies that the industry should use to make appropriate make/buy and strategic sourcing decisions with suppliers.

- PROFESSOR ANDREW COX, CHAIRMAN, ADVISORY BOARD, INTERNATIONAL INSTITUTE FOR ADVANCED PURCHASING & SUPPLY (IIAPS), FORMER DIRECTOR OF THE CENTRE FOR BUSINESS STRATEGY AND PROCUREMENT AT BIRMINGHAM UNIVERSITY BUSINESS SCHOOL, THE FIRST EVER MBA IN STRATEGIC PROCUREMENT MANAGEMENT.

Hedley's interesting exploration of SCM issues includes business, control, regulatory and technical aspects. The book is salted with many personal experiences which keep the reader entertained as well as informed. This book is a must read for those entering into the SCM fields as well as all those who intersect with SCM.

- BOB COLEMAN FORMER FDA NATIONAL EXPERT DRUG INVESTIGATOR

BOOKS BY THIS AUTHOR

Supply Chain Management In The Drug Industry

This book bridges the gap between practitioners of supply-chain management and pharmaceutical industry experts. It aims to help both these groups understand the different worlds they live in and how to jointly contribute to meaningful improvements in supply-chains within the globally important pharmaceutical sector. Scientific and technical staff must work closely with supply-chain practitioners and other relevant parties to help secure responsive, cost effective and risk mitigated supply chains to compete on a world stage. This should not wait until a drug has been registered, but should start as early as possible in the development process and before registration or clinical trials. The author suggests that CMC (chemistry manufacturing controls) drug development must reset the line of sight – from supply of drug to the clinic and gaining a registration, to the building of a patient value stream. Capable processes and suppliers, streamlined logistics, flexible plant and equipment, shorter cycle times, effective flow of information and reduced waste. All these factors can and should be addressed at the CMC development stage.

www.ingramcontent.com/pod-product-compliance
Lightning Source LLC
Chambersburg PA
CBHW072332290526
45794CB00002B/848